# lindbergh's artificial heart

## MORE FACINATING TRUE STORIES FROM EINSTEIN'S REFRIGERATOR

by steve silverman

**Andrews McMeel
Publishing**
Kansas City

03 04 05 06 07  EBI  10 9 8 7 6 5 4 3 2 1

Library of Congress Cataloging-in-Publication Data
Silverman, Steve, 1963–
Lindbergh's artificial heart : more fascinating true stories from
Einstein's refrigerator / by Steve Silverman.
    p. cm.
"The current volume . . . continues along the same lines as the
previous book"—Introd.
Includes bibliographical references.
ISBN 0-7407-3340-0
1. Curiosities and wonders. 1. Title.

AG243 .S564 2003
031.02—dc21

                                                2002040879

Book design by Holly Camerlinck

---

## Attention: Schools and Businesses

Andrews McMeel books are available at quantity discounts with bulk
purchase for educational, business, or sales promotional use.
For information, please write to: Special Sales Department,
Andrews McMeel Publishing, 4520 Main Street,
Kansas City, Missouri 64111.

# contents

# introduction

Welcome back! Since 1 am sure that you want to delve right in, 1 will keep my introductory comments to a minimum.

First, 1 must thank all my readers that made the last book, *Einstein's Refrigerator,* such a success. The current volume that you hold in your hands continues along the same lines as the previous book. This is a compilation of stories that pulls together some of the truly bizarre, highly creative, and long-forgotten pieces of human history. While some of these stories have appeared on my Web site, others are totally new and have not seen the light of day.

My research has always taken me down some unusual paths. Some were complete dead ends. The original working title for this book was "Henry Ford's Soybean Car," but 1 found myself reading too much literature written by hemp enthusiasts that happened to provide a brief mention of Ford's creation. 1 researched the stories "Fight!" "The 1904 Olympics," and "Ota Benga" independently of each other, but as more information unfolded over the years, 1 became aware that there were characters and situations central to all three. 1 also found myself taking a keen interest in the underdogs, like Philo Farnsworth, Reginald Fessenden, and Hannibal Goodwin. The similar struggle that each inventor faced while going up against the big boys is a situation that still rings true today.

Once again, 1 have chosen a conversational, humorous writing style. This book is all about having fun. Many people have told me that they love to read my stories in the bathroom, because each one is just long enough for one visit, if you know what 1 mean. . . . If my unusual sense of humor insults anyone, I apologize. That is certainly not my intention at all.

The address of my Web site was inadvertently left out of the previous edition. There are several mirror sites, but if you would like to read more, just point your Web browser to *www.einsteinsrefrigerator.com* or *www.uselessinformation.org*.

People have questioned why I end each story with "Useless? Useful? I'll leave that for you to decide." The reason is actually quite simple. When I started my Web site years ago, I gave it the name Useless Information. Every once in a while, someone would write in about one of their favorite characters and complain that I had called the person useless. In an effort to avoid insulting readers, I added those few words to the end of each story. If Ripley can state "Believe it or not!" on every page, the inclusion of my little comment once per story should fit right in.

Whether you are flipping the lid on your favorite drink or the porcelain prince, I hope that you enjoy what you are about to read.

Have fun!

## PART 1

# uh, oh!

# the flubber fiasco

## you just can't keep a good toy down

Flub·ber *(n.):* from the term *flying* rubber. A viscous, gooey green blob that defies the laws of physics and makes basketball players bounce and cars fly.

So much for definitions.

Now, I'm sure that you have probably seen one of the *Flubber* movies. This stuff was first "invented" by Fred MacMurray in the film *The Absent-Minded Professor* way back in March 1961. (Was this around the time that dinosaurs roamed the earth?) The movie made Disney so much money that it decided to make a sequel: *Son of Flubber* in 1963. And, not to let a good thing die, Disney released *Flubber* in 1997, a remake starring Robin Williams.

All good movies today have tons of product tie-ins. Remember the merchandising onslaught of *The Lion King*? *Lion King* dolls. *Lion King* drinking glasses. *Lion King* clothing. *Lion King* stickers. *Lion King* . . . well, you get the idea.

Of course, the latest incarnation of *Flubber* was no exception to this marketing blitz. Flubber seemed to be everywhere at just about the time Disney geared up to release its latest incarnation of the rubbery substance.

What few people know, however, is that there was a somewhat less successful tie-in attempted when *Son of Flubber* was released back in 1963. In fact, it may possibly be one of the most bizarre stories in all of toy history.

The product, of course, was named Flubber, and it was marketed by a toy manufacturer known as Hassenfeld Brothers (better known today as Hasbro). This particular formulation of Flubber was a mixture of rubber and mineral oil and had properties similar to that of Silly Putty. In other words, it bounced like a ball and could make comic imprints.

The product was introduced in September 1962 and Hasbro sold millions of units. The company advertised that "Flubber is a new parent-approved material that is nontoxic and will not stain."

But then, reports started to come back that some children were developing full-body rashes and sore throats from the product. The Food and Drug Administration (FDA) began investigating the product to see if these claims were true.

The bigwigs at Hasbro were mystified. The product was supposed to be harmless and had passed all of their safety tests.

In March 1963, a Kansas woman filed a $104,000 lawsuit against Hasbro, claiming that the Flubber had caused rashes so severe that both she and her three-year-old son required hospital care.

The company decided to retest the product. Instead of testing it on kids, Hasbro ended up using prisoners who volunteered to be guinea pigs. One prisoner developed a rash on his head. Why he was rubbing the Flubber on his head, one will never know, but it became clear that there was a problem with the product. It seems that the Flubber could irritate the hair follicles in a very small percentage of the human population.

What to do? What to do?

By May, over 1,600 complaints had been received (although some were for similar products made by other companies). Hasbro had no choice but to issue a voluntary recall. About 3 million Flubber balls were returned to the company. Then came the big question: Just what do you do with a huge mass of reject Flubber?

The obvious answer was to incinerate it. This seemed like a good idea until a huge black cloud formed and blocked out the sun in the region surrounding the local incinerator. While the Flubber could be bounced, it was clear that it shouldn't be burned. Hasbro had a big mess on its hands.

*And back to Hasbro the Flubber went. . . .*

It was decided that the balls should be trucked off and given a proper burial in the city dump. This also seemed like a good idea, until Hasbro received a call from city officials that kids were breaking into the dump and stealing it.

*And back to Hasbro the Flubber went. . . .*

Hasbro's next step was to do something that would be highly illegal today. The company decided to dump the balls into a large northern New England lake. Workers drove to the secluded lake and started to dump case after case of the Flubber into the water. They quickly learned that Flubber floats. Two fishing schooners were rented and it took four days of "fishing" to catch the estimated 50,000 Flubber balls.

*And back to Hasbro the Flubber went. . . .*

Hasbro's next solution was to bury the stuff in its own backyard. The process was very simple: (1) Dig a big hole. (2) Pour in a truckload of the Flubber. (3) Cover that with a truckload of sand. (4) Squash it all down with a steamroller. (5) Repeat steps 1 to 4 until all of the Flubber is buried. The Flubber burial ground was then paved over and made into a corporate parking lot.

One would guess that this was the end of the Flubber fiasco, but it was not.

Fast-forward forty years or so to the present. Hasbro employees claim that on a hot summer day, the Flubber actually oozes up through the cracks in the parking lot pavement. Probably just their imagination, but then this stuff did seem to take on a life of its own.

Useless? Useful? I'll leave that for you to decide.

# the great toilet paper shortage

## blame it all on johnny carson

There have been shortages of many things throughout history—oil, rubber, coffee, medicine, and so on. One of the most interesting shortages was the shortage of toilet paper, which was one that never needed to occur.

Before telling this unusual story, let's first take a quick look at the history of toilet paper.

Obviously, toilet paper has not been around forever. We can be pretty sure that the caveman did not stop at his local megasuperstore to pick up a case pack of Charmin. It is believed that the original materials used for cleaning (to put it politely) were leaves and sticks.

Of course, where you lived helped determine the material of choice. Mussel shells were very popular in coastal regions. If you were lucky enough to be raised on the Hawaiian Islands, you may have used good old coconut shells. If you were born into royalty, like Louis XIV, you would have used wool or lace for added comfort. In ancient Rome, all public toilets had a sponge attached to the end of a stick that was soaked in a bucket of brine. Rich Romans used wool and rose water.

The material of choice among colonial Americans was corncobs. When daily newspapers became commonplace in the 1700s, paper became the chosen favorite. (I guess you could say that Gutenberg's printing press caused the toilet paper revolution.) Lord Chesterfield (1694–1773) wrote in a letter to his son that he should always carry a cheap copy of the Latin poets. This would provide him with something educational to read while on the pot, as well as a good use for each page after reading it. This piece of advice led to a major problem in England: The landscape was littered with paper because they didn't have modern sewers to take the stuff away from sight.

In the late nineteenth century, the Sears catalog became popular in rural America. People simply hung it up on a nail and had a free supply of hundreds of pages of absorbent, uncoated paper. Corncobs were still holding as a strong second-place contender. Use of the Sears catalog declined in the 1930s because it was then printed on glossy, clay-coated paper. Many people complained to Sears about this glossy paper. (Imagine writing a letter to Sears: "Dear Sir, I want to register a complaint about your new glossy catalog paper. It is no longer soft and absorbent.")

The first actual paper produced for wiping was in England in 1880. It was individual squares sold in boxes, not rolls. This paper was very coarse, although it is hard to imagine that it could have been any worse than the stuff they provide in most public rest rooms today. The soft, fluffy type was introduced in 1907. The original American product was sort of like crepe paper, if you remember that stuff from kindergarten.

To make this background information complete, some statistics are needed. I should warn you that these statistics are a bit grotesque and are based only on a sample population of 106 people.

Here we go:

- The average tear is 5.9 sheets of TP.
- Forty-four percent wipe from front to back from behind their backs.
- Sixty percent look at the paper after they wipe.
- Forty-two percent fold; 33 percent crumple; 8 percent both fold and crumple; 6 percent wrap it around their hands.
- Fifty percent say they have wiped with leaves.
- Eight percent have wiped with their hands.

- Two percent have wiped with money! (An act of desperation?)

Which finally brings us back to our lead story—"The Great Toilet Paper Shortage!"

It actually all started as a joke. Johnny Carson was doing his typical NBC *Tonight Show* monologue on December 19, 1973.

*Heeeere's Johnnnnnny. . . .*

Of course, Johnny, like most talk show hosts, had a staff that helped write his monologues. His writers had heard earlier in the day about a Wisconsin congressman named Harold Froehlich. Froehlich claimed that the federal government was falling behind in getting bids to supply toilet paper and that "the United States may face a serious shortage of toilet tissue within a few months."

Carson's writers decided to include a joke based on this quote in his monologue. He said, "You know what's disappearing from the supermarket shelves? Toilet paper. There's an acute shortage of toilet paper in the United States."

Too bad they couldn't see the consequences of this statement. You may not be aware of this if you are young, but the early 1970s was a time of shortages, oil in particular. The next morning, many of the nation's 20 million television viewers ran to the supermarket and bought all the toilet paper they could find. By noon, most of the stores were out of stock. Stores tried to ration the stuff, but they couldn't keep up with the demand.

Johnny Carson went on the air several nights later and explained that there was no shortage and apologized for scaring the public. Unfortunately, people saw all the empty shelves in the stores, so the stampede continued.

Scott Paper showed video of its plants in full production and asked consumers to stay calm; there was no shortage. The video was of little help. The panic fed itself and continued.

Shelves were finally restocked three weeks later and the shortage was over. It is the only time in American history that the consumer actually created a major shortage. (I don't think that the "shortage" of Barbie or Power Ranger dolls at Christmas could be classified as a real shortage.)

One last thing. I have been asked many times over the years which way the toilet paper should be mounted on the dispenser. My friend Jamie insists that the loose end should hang from the back of the roll. Most people actually have the roll mounted so that the paper comes over the front. I honestly couldn't care less, but the next time you are in a gag gift shop, look at the rolls of toilet paper that are there. Whether they have printed crossword puzzles or bogus money on the paper, the image is always on the outside of the roll. The only way to insert this in your dispenser at home so that it can be seen properly is with the loose end coming down the front of the roll. Of course, one ingenious inventor finally came up with the perfect solution. He created a wall-mounted dispenser that rotates. If you don't like the way the roll is hanging, just rotate the dispenser 180 degrees and everything will be just fine.

Such problems . . .

Useless? Useful? I'll leave that for you to decide.

# "fight!"

## why you should never scream that word in a crowded room

I'm sure that you remember that wise rule that they taught you when you were growing up: Don't ever scream *"Fire!"* in a crowd. History has certainly shown time and time again that death can result if this rule is ignored.

I bet, however, that no one ever told you that you shouldn't scream *"Fight!"* in a crowded room.

Why?

The answer is quite simple: The Shiloh Baptist Church disaster provides all the proof ever needed.

To find out what happened during this disaster, we must set our timepieces back to September 19, 1902, and make a visit to this brand-new church located in Birmingham, Alabama.

The church was packed to capacity. Over 2,000 people had gathered for the National Convention of Negro Baptists to hear the famous Booker T. Washington give his address. Just as Mr. Washington finished his speech, a Baltimore lawyer named Judge Billou started an argument with the church's choir leader over an unoccupied seat. One of the choir members screamed, *"A fight!"* to the crowd.

This was a big mistake. A really *big* mistake.

It seems that the crowd mistook the word *fight* for *fire.*

In one mad rush, the congregation ran for the door. Unfortunately, 2,000 people can't fit through one door at the same time. People were trampled to death as they fell to the floor. Others suffocated because of the massive crush of people pushing against the church's outer walls.

In an effort to calm the crowd down, one of the ministers went to the lectern and pleaded for people to be quiet. Again the crowd thought that he said, "Fire!"

The floor of the church was approximately fifteen feet above street level. A set of long steps dropped from the church lobby to the sidewalk below. Unfortunately, the steps were flanked by high brick walls on either side.

You can see where this story is going. . . .

The people running out of the church pushed others down the steps. The staircase, with its confining walls, subsequently became another trap. Bodies began to pile up and many in the crowd suffocated under the mad rush. Others were luckier (if you can call it that) and only suffered from broken limbs and internal injuries. In the end, 115 people were trampled or suffocated to death.

So the next time you are about to scream, *"A fight!"* think twice about what the consequences could be.

Useless? Useful? I'll leave that for you to decide.

# the exploding whale

## son of blubber takes flight

For years, I have been keeping a file folder filled with information on one of the most peculiar stories that I have ever encountered. The two words on the folder's label, *Exploding Whale*, serve as a constant reminder to me of how one's good intentions can sometimes lead to disastrous results.

To begin, we must put this story into some sort of historical context. Versions of this event have been circulating around the Internet for several years, and they all imply that it happened recently. The reality is that the explosion took place way back on November 12, 1970. The mind-altering 1960s were over, the Beatles were gone, and I was just a little tyke. (In other words, I don't remember anything from that time.)

On that day, a forty-five-foot, eight-ton Pacific gray whale had recently washed onto the beach (big shock, huh?) just south of Florence, Oregon. Unfortunately, this whale had seen better days. To put it bluntly, this was one big, stinky corpse sitting up on the beach. The surf had tossed rotting pieces of it all over the shoreline. Definitely not the kind of thing that I would want to stand downwind from.

The question then arose as to who would clean up the mess. (You wouldn't find me volunteering for this job.) While the oceans may not look like the highways of today, at one time they provided the world's major routes of commerce. As a result, the job of getting rid of the whale fell into the hands of the Oregon State Highway Division.

So, let's suppose that you were working at the highway department there, and you were pressed to find a solution to the problem of getting rid of a big whale corpse. As a highway department employee, you would clearly see that getting rid of this monstrous carcass was not very different from removing a giant boulder from a road. The whale would clearly need to be blown up. A little explosive placed just right and the whale would be blown to smithereens, with all of the pieces flying out to sea. The fish and the seagulls would have a marvelous feast.

Unfortunately, all great plans are not executed as originally conceived. (If they were, I wouldn't be writing this story.) The highway department knew a great deal about removing dense boulders, but once-living flesh was another story. As crowds gathered on the nearby dunes, the highway crew placed twenty 50-pound cases of dynamite under the cadaver. One could smell the excitement in the air. (Okay, you've got me. We know that they couldn't smell the excitement. It just sounds better than smelling rotten whale.)

*Boom!*

As expected, the whale was blown to pieces. The chunks of blubber and tons of sand shot up into the sky in a giant reddish plume.

The spectators then got an added bonus. Instead of the pieces flying out over the ocean, they flew inland toward the dunes. All of a sudden, it began to rain rotten whale. Yuck! Make that a double "Yuck!" (Yuck! Yuck!!) Panic set in and people ran off in all directions screaming at the top of their lungs. (Images of a bad *Godzilla* movie come to mind.)

Luckily, not a single person was hurt. Sure, they smelled awful and were in need of a good bath, but not a single human limb was broken. One can also be sure that the seagulls, at least, did get their yummy meal, as originally planned.

A businessman named Walter Umenhofer may have walked away with his life, but his brand-new gold '98 Olds didn't fair as well. A large piece of the whale, measuring approximately three by five feet, flew over the crowd and landed right on top of his car, which was parked nearly a quarter of a mile away. The roof of his vehicle was crushed by the incredible momentum of the flying blubber. (Can you imagine calling your insurance company and reporting this accident? "You see, my car was hit by a piece of flying whale!. . . .")

A six-foot fin from the whale went for an even longer flight. It flew right over Umenhofer's car and headed toward another vehicle, where a baby was asleep in the backseat. It just missed the car and landed in a nearby marsh. It actually took a front-end loader to remove the fin from that quagmire.

In the end, the highway crew cleaned up the mess and buried what remained of the whale. The stench dissipated over a period of two months. The state ended up paying the full retail value of Umenhofer's car, and he was able to purchase a new one. It was also determined that the explosives had actually gone off just as planned, except that they funneled into the sand under the whale, instead of up into it.

Being the educated creatures that we are, we like to believe that we learn from our mistakes. When a pod of forty-one sperm whales was beached in nearly the same spot in 1979, the thought of using explosives was quickly ruled out. This time, the responsibility of cleanup fell into the hands of the State Parks Division. They chose to burn and bury the corpses.

Wise move . . .

Useless? Useful? I'll leave that for you to decide.

# the peshtigo fire

## you've never heard of it because a cow stole the spotlight

You know exactly which cow I am talking about. Mrs. O'Leary's cow. That darn cow that supposedly kicked over the lantern and burned Chicago to the ground. There is no real proof that the cow actually did it, but in our minds she will always be guilty of the crime. That October 8, 1871, fire destroyed some 17,500 buildings and caused an estimated $200 million in property damage. Approximately 300 people were killed and tens of thousands were left homeless.

Yet, on that very day of the Chicago disaster, another fire erupted that killed many more people and consumed more than 500 times more acreage. You have probably never heard of this fire, so you must be wondering where it occurred. Was it China, Africa, or Australia? No, it was right here in the United States, just 220 miles north of Chicago, in Peshtigo, Wisconsin. And, because of the attention placed by the history books on that clumsy cow, the worst fire in American history, at least in terms of loss of life, is basically forgotten today.

At the time, Peshtigo was a booming lumber town. Approximately 2,000 people lived in Peshtigo and more than 300 worked in its woodenwares factory producing tubs, buckets, and the like.

The spring and summer of 1871 were particularly dry through-out the entire northern frontier. Rainfall was considerably below the norm and a strong southwesterly wind produced increased evapora-tion. Swamps and wells dried up and the grass was like tinder. In other words, the weather was ripe for a great fire.

Small fires had been popping up in the region for many weeks. On the evening of October 8, things in Peshtigo took a very bad turn. A tornado of fire sprang up from nowhere. Its accompanying hurricane-force winds toppled chimneys and tore the roofs right off homes and businesses. Flames shot up above the tallest trees. Cinders and sparks flew in all directions. The inferno of hot air, filled with sand, ash, smoke, and dust, was not fit to breathe.

Panic ensued. Men, women, children, and animals all fled for their lives. But there was no place to go. The flames were everywhere. Hundreds of people crowded into the Peshtigo River, but the air above it seemed to be on fire. Others attempted to cross the wooden bridge to the other side of the river, only to discover that the people on the other side had the same idea in mind. Some people sought shelter down the shafts of their dried-out wells.

Bird's-eye view of Peshtigo, Wisconsin, in September 1871. The town was destroyed on October 8, 1871, by the deadliest fire in U.S. history. (Library of Congress)

Within one hour, the entire town of Peshtigo was gone and so was a large portion of its population. Some of its citizens had been trampled to death. It was reported that a number of people just burst into flames from the heat while on their way to the river. Others on the bridge died when it caught fire and collapsed into the river below. Those that sought shelter in the water were forced to stay there for five to six hours. Even with all the heat of the fire, many died from exposure to the cold river water. Many others were crippled for life.

To this day, no one really knows what the final death toll was. Too many bodies were reduced to ashes and entire families were wiped out. It has been estimated that some 1,200 to 1,500 people lost their lives to the inferno. Two-thirds were from Peshtigo itself and the remainder from its surrounding areas. Only 383 of the bodies were ever positively identified. One mass grave in Peshtigo contains the bodies of an estimated 350 unidentified victims.

Over 1 million acres of land were burned before the flames died down. The material damage was estimated to be in the millions of dollars. It was later reported that 27 schoolhouses, 9 churches, 959 homes, 1,028 barns and stables, and numerous farm animals were obliterated along the fire's entire path. Railroad magnate William Ogden, owner of Peshtigo's woodenwares plant, lost over $3 million between the Peshtigo and Chicago fires. The frame of only one building, which had been under construction at the time, actually survived the fire. It was scorched, but the high moisture content of its green wood prevented it from igniting.

Since everything was burned to the ground, news of the fire and its great death toll was slow to reach the outside world. Even when it did, the Great Chicago Fire had already captured the attention of the rest of the U.S. population. Little relief came in, and the governor of Wisconsin was forced to issue a proclamation that basically begged for some of the aid to be diverted from Chicago to the victims of the Peshtigo disaster. Eventually, some assistance did come, but it was nothing in comparison to what Chicago received.

Today, little is remembered about the greatest tragedy of its kind in U.S. history. It is barely mentioned in literature and little real evidence of it actually exists. A local museum has some charred wood, a metal pie plate, and a few singed Bibles, but that's about it.

If only that cow had not stolen the spotlight . . .

Useless? Useful? I'll leave that for you to decide.

# the horrors of dhmo

## this stuff is just downright scary

There is a tendency for those that are famous or have a large following to use their position as a pulpit. I don't claim to move in the same league as those people, but with the high readership of my Web site, it would be remiss of me not to bring to your attention one of the scariest chemicals that I have ever come across.

This particular compound is known as dihydrogen monoxide, or DHMO, for short. DHMO does occur naturally, but man has managed to produce large amounts of it as a by-product of our modern industrialized society. As a major component of acid rain, scientists believe that DHMO has managed to infiltrate every stream, lake, and ocean worldwide.

DHMO is a colorless, odorless, and tasteless chemical that is responsible for the deaths of thousands of people each year. Accidental inhalation is a leading cause of death due to DHMO. Prolonged exposure to it can produce serious tissue damage. Many people each year suffer from serious burns because of contact with DHMO. Current research has found DHMO in the tumors of terminal cancer patients.

Mankind uses DHMO in many ways. It is a major ingredient in industrial solvents and coolants, is needed for the production of Styrofoam, is used as a fire retardant, and is widely used as an agent to distribute pesticides. In fact, DHMO is a component of a number of caustic, explosive, and poisonous compounds.

Scared yet? It only gets worse. . . .

DHMO has even found its way into our food and our drinking water. Dairy farmers feed it to their cows in massive quantities to increase milk production. As a result, nearly every gallon of milk available in the supermarket today contains DHMO, although a handful of companies are now manufacturing DHMO-free milk. Research has shown that DHMO is an excellent preservative of vegetables and it is used widely in supermarket produce sections. DHMO is also an additive in many shampoos, shaving creams, and bathroom cleansers.

I have been telling my students about DHMO for years and they have always reacted with horror. That is why I have decided that it is important to let you know. But there is something that you can do to help. Write to your elected representatives and let them know that you want DHMO banned. Let them know about your concerns. Mail them letters of protest; sign petitions; get your community involved. There is a lot that you can do before it is too late.

But wait! Think carefully before you leap. As I mentioned earlier, DHMO is short for dihydrogen monoxide. That is two hydrogen atoms and one oxygen atom combined into a molecule. Does that sound even remotely familiar? Have you ever heard of water?

Useless? Useful? I will leave that for you to decide.

# the creative mind at work

# the matchstick man

## the most unusual instrument collection in the world

Don't you just feel sorry for the match? Its useful life is just so short. It's brought to life with just one flick of the stick and then—poof!— the match's life is over in an instant. This seems like such a complete waste. Every year, we probably dispose of tons upon tons of these things. Could a matchstick recycling program be of some use here? Possibly, but what would we do with all of these things once we collected them all?

Unbeknownst to most people, one man came up with the perfect solution. He used burned wooden matchsticks to build musical instruments. Yes, you did read that correctly. He used those dinky little burned things to build guitars, banjos, and the like.

This ingenious man's name was Jack Hall. Back in the 1930s, Jack was a sailor aboard the tramp steamer *Eastwick* and found himself with just a little bit too much time on his hands. Bored out of his mind, Jack just started messing around with the discarded wooden matchsticks that his fellow sailors had left behind, eventually gluing them together into increasingly complex and fascinating patterns.

Jack's first project was nothing to write home to Mom about. It was a simple two-ply plank that was basically useless. But, it was a start. Like all hobbyists, as Jack's skills improved, his projects became larger and more complex. He applied his matchstick techniques to the design of boxes, a clock, a miniature windmill and lighthouse. All still relatively useless, but they were great to look at on a shelf.

Jack ran into a major problem. He couldn't get enough matches. (It's hard for me to believe that a boatload of sailors couldn't smoke enough cigarettes to keep Jack in supply!) Jack had to seek alternative sources and began to ask his friends and family to save any burned matchsticks that they could get their hands on. Each time that his ship pulled into port, Jack would stock up.

It was the offhand comment made by a fellow sailor that he should "make a fiddle and strike up a tune," however, that sent Jack off into the world of matchstick music. Jack's curiosity had gotten the better of him, and he was determined to make that fiddle a reality. But Jack lacked some key skills to pull this trick off. First, he was not a musician. He couldn't read or play a single note. Even worse, Jack did not have any of the carpentry skills needed to produce an instrument.

Clearly, this lack of skills did not stop Jack, so let's continue our story:

Each time his ship stopped in port, Jack would visit local music stores and pawnshops to study the various aspects of the violin. He recorded all the necessary measurements and made rough pencil sketches of the instrument to take back to sea with him.

For the next six months, Jack devoted five hours a day to his creation. He used little more than a sharp knife, a razor blade, some sandpaper, a file, and glue. Each matchstick was soaked in water so it could be molded into the proper shape. Bricks and other heavy objects were used to hold the matchsticks in place while the glue set.

Some 14,000 matchsticks later, Jack produced a working violin, bow and all. You're probably sitting there with an image of a cheap, flimsy instrument in your mind. Instead, Jack's violin looked as elegant as the best of violins. But, the real question was whether or not it would actually play. Jack, with his little bit of musical skill, was able to crank out a few screeches, but the real test of the instrument's quality would have to wait.

Jack wasn't content to stop with the violin. Between 1936 and 1939, he expanded his collection, which grew to include two mandolins, a tenor banjo, and an acoustic guitar. Not only did he build the instruments, but he also created a carrying case for each one. The cases, get this, were made from the actual boxes that the matches were sent to him in. The instrument cases were painted the traditional black on the outside, but upon opening, one would encounter a dizzying array of matchbox logos and images. Unintentionally, each case uniquely captured a snapshot of history.

Hobbies of this magnitude require something that so many of us seem to lack these days: time. With the onset of World War II, Jack found himself in a similar situation. By the time of his military discharge in 1945, he had all but abandoned his craft. Over the next forty years, he was able to add only a recorder and a ukulele to his collection.

Excluding a brief exhibition in 1951 at the Festival of Great Britain, Jack's instruments rarely saw the light of day. This all changed in 1976, when a reporter/musician from BBC Radio Brighton heard about Jack's collection. Jack pulled the instruments out of his attic and dusted them off. They were in perfect working order and sounded superb.

It would not be until 1991 that Jack's dream for these instruments would actually come true. His instruments were played by a quintet of professional musicians before a live audience on BBC Television. Not only did Jack get to see the instruments professionally played for the first time, but everyone was impressed by the amazing sound that they produced.

Sadly, Jack passed away in 1993 at the age of eighty-six. Jack's son Tony now cares for the twenty-six–piece matchstick collection, which includes thirteen

Jack Hall with a portion of the musical instrument collection that he crafted from matchsticks. (Courtesy of Tony Hall)

musical instruments, the windmill, the lighthouse, and Jack's other creations.

Musicians continue to marvel at this unique collection. Most recently, this treasure appeared in an episode of *Ripley's Believe It or Not!* It featured the Rhinestone Cowboy himself, Glen Campbell, playing Jack's 1937 guitar. Glen stated, "It's a marvelous work of art and as good as any instrument that I've played of this era." At son Tony's request, Glen performed "Amazing Grace" for the segment. It was dedicated to Jack's wife, Tony's mom, who was struggling with the final stages of terminal cancer at the time. Mom was certainly proud and filled with delight. We can be sure that Jack was looking down from above with equal pride and joy.

And to think that it all started from a few discarded matchsticks.

Useless? Useful? I'll leave that for you to decide.

# eveready batteries

## he gave the company away to work on model trains

The foolish man that gave Eveready away was Joshua L. Cowen, who was your typical turn-of-the-century inventor. He had lots of ideas, some that worked and some that didn't.

While a student at the Peter Cooper Institute high school, Cowen was able to explore his fascination with the developing world of electricity. He claimed to have invented the first electric doorbell, but his instructor advised him that it was a dead-end pursuit. Nothing could ever replace the pounding of one's hand against solid wood.

In 1893, at age sixteen, Cowen entered the College of the City of New York but soon dropped out. He then returned, quit again, entered Columbia University, and then quit after one semester. Clearly, the confines of a formal education were not in the cards for Joshua Cowen. Instead, he chose to apprentice at Henner & Anderson, one of the first companies in the United States to manufacture dry-cell batteries. He quickly moved into another apprenticeship at Manhattan's Acme Electric Lamp Company, where he was able to refine his electrical skills.

On June 6, 1899, Cowen filed a patent for his next invention, which was intended to revolutionize photography. He designed the "flash lamp," which contained a battery-operated fuse designed to ignite magnesium-powered flashes. The invention was a dud. His best customer turned out to be the U.S. Navy. The Navy, however, didn't want to take pictures with Cowen's fuses. It purchased 24,000 of them to detonate underwater mines. Cowen received $12,000 for his efforts, which was quite a hefty chunk of cash in those days.

Cowen used his newfound fortune to develop new products for his own company. One of these was the first portable electric fan. While the concept was great, the fan worked very poorly at creating a breeze. By the time it was perfected, the hot summer had ended, as did the market for Cowen's fan.

His next creation was the development of little metal tubes that were designed to illuminate plants and flowers in their pots. While of little practical use, these lights produced a great dramatic effect. There was some interest in the product, but the illuminated flowerpots were incredibly difficult to perfect. (If he could have gotten the lighted plants to dance to music, he would have earned a fortune.) Cowen became bored with his flowerpot lights and gave the project away to one of his salesmen—some guy named Conrad Hubert. Hubert couldn't care less about the lighted flowerpots. Instead, he liked the device Cowen had developed to operate them: a lightbulb-and-dry-cell-battery combination that had a thirty-day life.

Hubert took Cowen's battery-operated device and developed it into the flashlight. The company founded on the invention that Cowen gave away was named the American Eveready Company, and it earned Hubert nearly $6 million in two decades. (A huge sum of money at the turn of the century.) When Hubert died, he left behind a $15,000,000 estate, virtually all earned from Cowen's invention.

One would think that Cowen would have felt like a real loser by now. He'd invented the electric doorbell and dropped the idea on the advice of a shortsighted teacher. He'd invented a portable electric fan but missed the boat on that one. Even worse, he'd failed to see the potential for a battery-operated light and watched Hubert become a millionaire many times over.

Well, don't feel too sorry for Cowen just yet. In 1901, he actually came up with another idea, the one that would make him a fortune. What I failed to mention was that the L in Joshua L. Cowen's name stood for Lionel—as in Lionel trains.

When Cowen gave away his flowerpot light company, he turned his attention to the development of these electric toys. He had been walking around lower Manhattan one day trying to find a new use for his electric fan motor. All of a sudden, his eyes were drawn to the window of Robert Ingersoll's toy and novelty shop. The display was filled with the toys of the period, all motionless. Cowen rushed into the store and explained that he would like to put an electric train in the window. It would go round and round and draw customers into the store.

The first Lionel train that he produced for Ingersoll was a flatbed car that ran on batteries, since few homes or businesses had been wired for electricity at the time. While Cowen had only intended the trains for use in eye-catching window displays, he quickly found that people wanted them for their homes, particularly for under the Christmas tree.

And the rest is model-train history.

Useless? Useful? I'll leave that for you to decide.

# pez

## available in eucalyptus, peppermint, and chlorophyll flavors!

PEZ!

You must be living in a box if you are not familiar with this candy and its flip-top-head dispensers. Over 1 billion of these little bundles of compressed sugar are sold each year in the United States alone.

So where did this novel approach to selling candy come from?

To find out, we must take a trip back to Vienna, Austria, in 1927. Here we will find a candy man named Eduard Haas III. Surprisingly, Haas did not try to sell his candy to kids. His focus was on adults. In particular, adults that smoked cigarettes. PEZ was originally marketed as a compressed breath mint for smokers to cover up their bad breath.

I know what you are thinking: *How did those fruit-flavored pellets cover your bad breath?*

The answer is quite simple; they weren't fruit flavored back then!

In fact, they were peppermint flavored, which explains the origin of its unusual name. The German word for peppermint is P*feff*E*rmin*Z. From that was gleaned the acronym PEZ!

The first dispensers for these peppermint-flavored candies weren't introduced until the late 1940s and are now referred to as "regulars," since they lacked the character heads PEZ is famous for.

In 1952, it was time to come to America. Superman, Bozo the

Clown, and the rest of the PEZ clan boarded the *Mayflower* and landed at Plymouth Rock. Oh, sorry. Wrong story.

Actually, the company did extensive market research with American children that led to the introduction of the fruity flavors and character heads on the dispensers. Since then, over 275 different PEZ heads have been designed, with some 48 models on the market at any one time. The most popular dispensers of all time are the Mickey Mouse and Santa Claus models. When the Flintstones models were introduced several years ago, they quickly rose to become a hot seller, with Dino, the purple dinosaur, being in short supply.

Even more surprisingly, people actually pay big bucks for these things. The highest price ever paid was $3,600 for a rare Big Top Elephant, which was sold by David Welch in July 1995. It's hard to say whether your old PEZ dispenser is worth anything. Some research will be required, but you can be almost certain about one thing: If the PEZ dispenser has molded feet at the base, then it is generally not worth very much. These appendages started appearing on the scene in 1987 and collectors will snub their noses at these dispensers.

Today, you can purchase PEZ T-shirts, puzzles, yo-yos, neckties, necklaces, magnets, mouse pads, key chains, and a whole range of other PEZ-related products.

Technology has also played a part in the history of PEZ. For example, a company named Cap Toys makes the battery-powered Power PEZ, which twirls and shoots the candies into your mouth. Another company, Dream Castle, markets the PEZ watch, which dispenses the candies out the side of the watch.

Being an avid consumer of PEZ candies, I am limited to peppermint and the four fruit flavors available in the United States: grape, lemon, orange, and strawberry. Hop across the border to Canada, and you can add cherry to your stash. Raspberry and apple are available in Spain. Chocolate is available in Hungary and Thailand. The vitamin-enriched IZO PEZ is also available in Hungary. (Does a vitamin-enriched candy make sense to you?) The most unusual flavors, however, have to be the discontinued ones: chloro-phyll, cinnamon, coffee, cola, eucalyptus, flower (just what do flow-ers taste like?), licorice, and menthol. Just what were the marketing guys thinking of when they came up with some of these flavors?

Useless? Useful? I'll leave that for you to decide.

# pink flamingos

## so tacky, yet so cool

The pink flamingo is one of those objects that people seem to either love or hate. Considered by some to be a work of art and by others to be visual pollution, this one object stands for everything that is good and bad about our modern society.

Lawn ornaments are nothing new. From marble statues created centuries ago to the Granny Fannies of the late 1980s, lawn decorations have been around for an eternity. Some compare a lawn without any ornaments to a coffee table that is empty.

The history of the pink flamingo can be traced back to 1946 when a company called Union Products started manufacturing "plastics for the lawn." Its collection included dogs, ducks, frogs, and even flamingos. But its products had one problem: They were only two-dimensional.

Hmmm . . . World peace surely depended on solving this critical problem.

In 1956, the Leominster, Massachusetts, company decided to hire a young designer named Don Featherstone. Although Don was a serious sculptor and a classical art student, his first project was to redesign Union Products' popular duck into the third dimension. (One must do what one can to pay the bills.) Don used a live duck as his model, and after five months of work, the duck was retired to a local park.

His next project would prove to be his most famous. He couldn't get his hands on real flamingos, so he used photographs from a

*National Geographic* instead. He sculpted the original out of clay, and this was then used to make a plaster cast. The plaster cast, in turn, was used to form the molds for the plastic. The original design called for detailed wooden legs, but they proved to be too costly and were replaced by the metal ones still seen today. While the exact date was never recorded, the first pink flamingo was born sometime during 1957.

The late 1950s just happened to be perfect timing for the flamingo.

America was moving to the suburbs. Industry was convincing America that a natural lawn was one that was mowed and treated with chemicals. And, every lawn needed a lawn ornament.

But empty lawns weren't the only things in the flamingo's favor. The country was much more mobile, and an increasing number of people were traveling to the many hotels, motels, and lounges named after the flamboyant flamingo. The 1950s were also a time for bright, bold colors. Common colors had been around for years, but plastics now allowed for hot colors like bright green, vivid ruby, and, of course, hot flamingo pink. Pink refrigerators, washing machines, and Cadillacs were highly sought after.

The 1960s were not as friendly to the pink flamingo. There was a rebellion against everything man-made. It was a time to go back to nature. The plastic flamingo quickly became the prototype of bad taste and antinature. By 1970, even Sears had removed the pink-feathered bird from its catalog.

It looked like our fake feathered friend's days were numbered. But time was on this bird's side. Some people just love to do things that annoy other people. If pink flamingos were the ultimate in bad taste, then people were sure to place them on their lawns to bug their neighbors. And they did so in great numbers.

When I first started college back in 1981, I went to see a movie titled *Pink Flamingos*. My recommendation is that you never, ever, see this 1973 flick. It is the most disgusting movie ever made. You'll probably vomit long before it ends. Yet, this movie clearly marks the time that the pink flamingo moved from lawn junk to lawn art.

In 1984, *Miami Vice* kicked the sales of pink flamingos into full throttle. For the first time ever, Union Products sold more flamingos than they did ducks. Today, they are sold for just about every purpose. They are purchased for use as wedding decorations, as housewarming gifts, and as replacements for reindeer at Christmastime. Some people actually travel with their pink flamingos. The plastic birds go camping, hiking, skiing, and mountain biking. Entire Web sites are devoted to the travels of these artificial creatures.

Pink flamingos have also become a prime target of pranksters. Many are stolen off lawns every year, particularly by kids that have been drinking a wee bit too much. Others are kidnapped and held for ransom. One particular pair was kidnapped and had their ransom paid in play money.

We all know that what is art to one person is garbage to another. Bans have been placed on pink flamingos all over the country. As a result, Union Products was forced to introduce a blue flamingo to circumvent the rules. Of course, these communities then changed the laws to ban all plastic flamingos. (That's when I would paint my house purple.)

Should you wish to purchase these decorations, they are readily available. Hundreds of thousands are sold each year in stores and through mail order. Authentic flamingos always have Don Featherstone's signature under their tails. Each has a yellow beak with a black tip and they are only sold in pairs.

Useless? Useful? I'll leave that for you to decide.

# barbecuing

## who really needs lighter fluid?

In an effort to promote my first book, *Einstein's Refrigerator*, the publisher arranged a number of telephone interviews for me with various radio stations around the country. First, I must point out that if someone wants to give me free publicity, I'm game. Yet, if you ever get the opportunity to do the same, you will quickly notice that the time you spend doing an interview is inversely proportional to the number of listeners. If you are lucky enough to get on the air in a big market, they will give you ten minutes, at most. On the other hand, if you are scheduled to do an interview in some small town in the boonies, then you can be sure that you will be spending an hour with the host and his three listeners. But, I am not complaining. All it takes is one of those three listeners to talk to just the right person and . . .

Well, it was during one of my recent interviews that the story that I am about to tell came up. The host asked me if I had ever heard of the story of the MIT engineering professor that held a contest to see which one of his students could light a barbecue the fastest. One of the students apparently got carried away and decided to use liquid oxygen. He poured the really cold liquid onto the briquettes, threw in a lit cigarette, and—*kaboom!* The whole thing blew up. When the fire department finally showed up, all that was left of the professor and the student were their charcoal remains.

He asked me if the story was actually true. I honestly had no clue. I explained that many of these stories are rooted in truth but tend to take on lives of their own as word spreads. This story sounded a lot like an urban legend, but I figured I would check it out as soon as I got off the phone with him.

Now, as you probably already know, the Internet is filled with stories like this. I don't know why, but many of these things seem to take place at MIT or Harvard and the idiots almost always end up being toast. (The widely circulated, yet totally untrue, story about the fool who attached a solid-fuel rocket engine to the back of his car comes to mind.)

Yet, as I had suspected, there was some truth to this story. MIT was not involved, nor was there a contest, and no one was ever hurt. So now you are thinking that you should stop reading, huh? Surely, if no one died, it can't be that great of a tale. Well, you can stop here if you like, but I think that you may be interested in continuing.

The true part of this story goes back to 1995, when a Purdue University computer engineer named George Goble got his fifteen minutes of worldwide fame as the subject of a Dave Barry article. This recognition allowed George to go on and win the 1996 Ig Nobel Prize. If you have never heard of this award, it is probably for good reason. In an attempt to spoof the real Nobel Prize, this particular award is given annually for "achievements that cannot or should not be reproduced." (Make sure you heed these words carefully. Don't be the soon-to-be-dead-in-an-explosion birdbrain that decides to try this thing at home.)

Goble basically had the same problem that all of us grillers have had with a barbecue at some point in life. You just can't get the charcoal briquettes to light. You spray on some lighter fluid, light the match, and . . . nothing. Within ten seconds, you are squirting on more fluid and pulling out another match. (Sometimes I think that they may have mislabeled the can. Maybe they accidentally filled it with fire extinguisher fluid.)

Now, you may be asking, "Who was the crazy person that gave the world charcoal briquettes?" Believe it or not, it was good old

Henry Ford himself. He became obsessed with all of the raw materials being thrown out of his manufacturing plant, including all of the wood scraps and sawdust remaining after the running boards were installed in his cars. (Even the running boards in his woody station wagons were made of scrap. They were made from the shipping crates that the car parts came in.) Somehow, in Ford's mind, he saw a great market for flammable little chunks of carbon. The scrap wood was made into charcoal and then compressed into briquettes, although the flammable portion of the equation is still questionable. They were marketed as Ford Charcoal Briquettes (what else?) until 1951, when new ownership renamed them Kingsford Charcoal Briquettes. Just what was this guy thinking? If I could turn back the clock, I would give Mr. Ford some advice: Model T, good idea; charcoal briquettes, bad idea.

But, I have led you astray. Let's get back to our friend Mr. Goble. As mentioned above, George was just like the common man. He always struggled to get his briquettes to ignite. Over the years, George and some of his engineering pals came up with faster and faster schemes to get the barbecue to light. They started simply with a standard hair dryer. Their next step was to try a vacuum cleaner. Then it was a propane torch, then an acetylene torch, and then . . .

Well, you get the idea. Eventually, they had the coals burning in less than thirty seconds using a ten-foot pipe attached to a scuba diver's tank of oxygen.

Yet, George was still not satisfied. He just had to get that starting time down. He decided to use liquid oxygen. Now, you may not know what liquid oxygen is, but it doesn't take much of a genius to figure out that this stuff does not form naturally on planet Earth. No, it takes the ingenuity of mankind to produce this liquid. Just take some pure oxygen and get it really, really cold. That's around 297-degrees-below-zero (-183°C) cold, to be specific. (A tennis ball dipped in this stuff will shatter like glass when bounced.) What makes this stuff so great in the liquid form is that there are many more oxygen atoms in a given volume at this temperature. More oxygen means more *POW!* if you know what I mean.

George's technique was quite ingenious. First, he filled a really cheap grill (the reason for this will soon be obvious) with some sixty pounds of briquettes. Someone then flicked a lit cigarette onto the pile. A galvanized three-gallon bucket was then attached to a long handle. Liquid oxygen was dumped into the bucket, extended over the grill, and poured on the briquettes. Within three seconds, a 10,000-degree, blinding fireball had the barbecue cooking.

Without a doubt, lighting a barbecue so quickly does have its share of drawbacks. First, you could end up dead. Assuming that you are well insured and have decided to risk it all for the sake of impatience, you will still have to contend with the fact that the grill will be no more. Yes, the flame gets so hot that the grill will basically vaporize and you will have nothing left to cook on except some very hot coals lying on the ground. And, of course, if the grill can't survive the heat, neither will your food. Your hamburgers, hot dogs, and chicken will turn almost instantaneously into carbon.

Just be aware that George knew exactly what he was doing. You may not be as clever. Miss one important detail, and I can assure you that you will not be a happy camper. When the fire department comes to hose down what little remains of your home, your family, and your surrounding community, you may wish that you had not tried this scheme in the first place. Yes, you may just end up as a pile of carbon, which is exactly where this story started. MIT may never have played a part in your life, but all that the investigators will ever find of you is toast.

Useless? Useful? I'll leave that for you to decide.

# Lindbergh's artificial heart

## he was more than a famous pilot

A recent classroom discussion somehow led me to ask my ninth-grade students, "Who did we fight in the Civil War?" Nobody seemed to know. Answers included the British, the Japanese, the Germans, the Mexicans, and the Martians. Finally, after five minutes of wrong answers, one of my shyest students whispered the correct answer to me. I barely heard her, but she knew that the North had fought the South. After that experience, I decided to ask a similar question each day to find out what my students really knew. Only one of my twelfth-grade physics students actually knew who Lyndon Johnson was. Almost everyone thought that the majority of rivers in the Northern Hemisphere flowed south because that was "downhill." To their credit, nearly all of the students correctly answered "Who fought in World War III?"

Which leads us to the title subject of this book. Students today just seem to have no idea who Charles Lindbergh was. While most of the questions that I was throwing at them had an obvious twist or trick, I was sure that they would get this one right. They didn't. One student had a faint recollection that he had something to do with airplanes, but that was about it.

Now, I will spare you the in-depth details of the famous parts of Lindbergh's life. There are piles of books and articles written on the subject, and, hopefully, my brief overview will remind those who claim not to know that they really did learn something about this guy in school.

Born in Detroit in 1902, "Lucky Lindy" achieved worldwide fame by becoming the first man to solo an airplane across the Atlantic Ocean. He did this on May 20–21, 1927, in thirty-three and a half hours. For this accomplishment, he was showered with tons of honors, awards, celebrations, and parades. His custom designed plane, *Spirit of St. Louis*, is still one of the focal points of the Smithsonian National Air and Space Museum in Washington, D.C.

Sadly, fame brought unintended consequences. On March 1, 1932, Lindbergh's firstborn son, Charles junior, was kidnapped from his home nursery. On May 12, he was found brutally murdered. The trial and execution of the murderer, Bruno Hauptmann, brought incredible publicity to the Lindbergh couple. To escape the glare of the spotlight, Lindbergh and his wife, Anne, picked up and moved to England.

These are the two stories that are discussed most frequently when the name Charles Lindbergh is mentioned. Yet, the one that intrigues me most is the one that is barely mentioned at all. That is the story of what was to become known in the press as "Lindbergh's artificial heart."

In 1929, Anne's older sister, Elisabeth Morrow, developed a lesion in her heart after a bout with pneumonia. As a result of this heart damage, she was instructed to minimize physical activity and was warned that the length of her life would be shortened—certainly not news that anyone wants to hear. Lindbergh asked the doctors why cardiac surgery was out of the question. He was told that there was no known way to operate on the heart without stopping circulation to the rest of the patient's body for a lengthy period of time.

Lindbergh knew very little about heart surgery, but it seemed clear in his mind that all that was needed was a mechanical pump that could circulate the blood while the heart was being worked on. And, he theorized, "Why could not the entire body be kept alive after the heart it is born with becomes too old and worn out to function?" The idea of an artificial heart was born. He was certain that his idea couldn't be original, yet doctor after doctor informed him that they had never heard of such a pump being used during surgery.

Lindbergh, Carrel, and their heart pump on the June 13, 1938, cover of *Time* magazine. (Library of Congress)

On the night of the birth of Charles junior, Lindbergh was in a small room waiting with the obstetrician, Dr. Hawks, and the anesthetist, Dr. Flagg. Once again, he brought up the question of his idea for a heart pump. They could not offer him any information, but Dr. Flagg agreed to arrange a meeting between Lindbergh and a man that he thought might have the answers.

At a luncheon at the Rockefeller Institute for Medical Research, Lindbergh was intro-duced to the head of the insti-tute's Department of Experimental Surgery, Dr. Alexis Carrel. Carrel was a Nobel Prize–winning pioneer in the field of vascular surgery and was on the forefront of organ transplantation. He had been working for many years on a way to keep organs alive for long periods outside the body but had been unsuccessful in creating a circulating pump to do this.

Lindbergh looked at the equipment that Carrel had created and was sure that he could greatly improve on the designs. The two men struck up what would appear to be a totally mismatched friendship, but it worked well. Lindbergh's earliest pump designs worked, but they were far from satisfactory. In April 1935, after five years of redesign, building, and testing, they had successfully cultivated the thyroid of a cat. This was the first time in history that a complete organ had been kept in vitro. Their research culminated with the joint publication of *The Culture of Organs* in 1938.

Unfortunately, World War II would bring an end to their collab-oration. Carrel died during the war from heart failure. (If only they had gotten that pump perfected sooner. . . .) Lindbergh flew combat missions over the Pacific, but his isolationist and seemingly prejudicial wartime views brought him into extreme public disfavor. After the war, he retreated from public view until his death in 1974.

"And what about Elisabeth Morrow, the woman that inspired Lindbergh to develop the heart pump?" you may ask. Her doctors' predictions were correct and her life was ultimately cut short. She died in 1934 of what was termed "natural causes."

Many attribute the Lindbergh artificial heart and its associated research with laying the foundation for modern cardiovascular surgery. While the use of heart-lung machines during surgery was still many years away, one can't help but be thankful for the vision and effort that Lindbergh put into making them a reality much earlier.

Useless? Useful? I will leave that for you to decide.

# philo farnsworth

## how one boy changed the world

For the past several years, I have served on our local PBS television station's Educational Services Committee. A while back, I was asked by the station to attend a state conference on the role of digital television in the classrooms of tomorrow. The conference was well attended, but, strangely enough, I was the only teacher there.

The guest speaker was a former CEO of the RCA Corporation, a man whose name I have purposely forgotten. His whole speech centered on the fact that RCA had single-handedly invented television. On and on he went about RCA's great achievement. The woman that I attended the conference with could see that I was a bit annoyed by the whole bit. Just the previous night, I had been telling her the real history of television, and what this guy was saying was just plain wrong.

My story, which you know is going to be totally different from that ex-RCA bigwig's, starts in Indian Creek, Utah, on August 19, 1906. On this day, a boy named Philo Taylor Farnsworth was brought into the world and would eventually be the oldest of five children. As all stories of great men go, he lived in near poverty in a log cabin without any modern conveniences.

When Philo was twelve, the Farnsworth family picked up roots and moved to a small ranch in the Snake River Valley of Idaho in search of more fertile farmland. Their new home had a convenience that they had never experienced before: that newfangled thing called electricity. Philo took an instant interest in the flow of these mighty electrons. In the attic of the new home, he discovered piles of science and radio magazines. (Keep in mind that radio was brand new at the time.) Philo read these magazines from cover to cover, absorbing all of the new knowledge that he could. He then read them over and over again.

In the fall of 1921, Philo enrolled in the local high school, but the courses were not challenging enough for him. As a freshman, he was taking senior chemistry, but even this proved to be too simplistic for this young man's eager mind. His chemistry teacher, Justin Tolman, provided him with additional tutoring after school each day.

During the winter of 1922, as young Philo continued his studies of the latest electronic magazines, he came across an article on something called television. It was basically a dream at the time to somehow splice the images of movies with the sound of radio and transmit them through the air. Yet, some scientists were making a little headway in this area. Using a complex system of spinning disks, experimental television broadcasts were already underway. The most famous of these men was a man named John Logie Baird, who actually sent the first transatlantic TV signal in 1928 and had an operating television network in Britain in the late 1920s.

Philo's gut reaction was that this mechanical system of television could never work. These beasts were just too difficult to calibrate and their resolution was very poor. He figured that if he could harness the power of the electron, he could solve the problem.

Of course, the real question was how to do this.

The answer hit Philo one day while he was plowing the family's potato field at the tender age of just fourteen. As he took the plow back and forth across the field, he couldn't help but notice the parallel tracks left behind. In simplistic terms, what Philo quickly realized was that if he could get a beam of electrons to move back and forth row by row, he could generate a television image without any moving parts.

He had a great idea, but with whom could he share his excitement?

There was only one man that Philo knew who could understand his concept. That was Justin Tolman, his chemistry teacher. Once

Philo perfected the fundamental design of the system, he took it to school and, drawing a long series of diagrams on the chalkboard, explained the whole thing to Tolman. Yes, a teenager had just laid down the blueprints for electronic television, the same system that is in use in nearly every household today.

Surely someone must have stumbled onto this idea. But Philo knew that the researchers of the day were simply barking up the wrong tree. Industry just had it plain wrong. He would later find out that he was not the only person in the world with the same idea, but we'll hold off on that for a while.

Of course, having a good idea and making it a reality are two totally different things. The Farnsworth family moved back to Utah, and Philo was accepted as an early admission to Brigham Young University. With the vast resources that the university had to offer, Philo was finally able to do his own research into the nature of the cathode-ray tube and the electrons it produced. Sadly, Philo's dad contracted pneumonia and died just before the Christmas of 1923. Philo's formal education was brought to a sudden end when he was only eighteen.

In 1925, Phil, as he now preferred to be known, met up with George Everson and Leslie Gorrell, who were in Salt Lake City to raise money for a community chest program. Phil secured a temporary job with Everson and during an after-dinner conversation one day, discussed his idea for electronic television. Everson and Gorrell were hooked and wanted in on the development. Together, the two men invested $6,000, which was a lot of dough in those days. One stipulation to their agreement was that Phil had to relocate to Los Angeles to do the research. Figuring that L.A. offered better resources, he agreed. Phil married his sweetheart, Pem, and they moved off to the big city right away.

Once in Los Angeles, things were not as easy as one would think. Keep in mind that since television hadn't yet been invented, you couldn't just head down to your local RadioShack for spare parts. Virtually everything had to be made from scratch. After three months of experimentation, Phil and his lab team were ready for their first test. The tension in the room mounted. The power switch was flipped. Electrons surged into the device.

*Boom!*

The generator blew the whole thing up. Three months of work right down the drain.

The initial capital that Everson and Gorrell put up was quickly gone and another $25,000 was secured from an additional group of investors. In return for their investment, Phil assured them he would have a picture for them within one year.

So, did he meet his self-imposed deadline?

Of course he did. On September 7, 1927, the redesigned system was ready for its first run. Phil, Pem, and Everson gathered in one room of the lab. Pem's brother Cliff was in another room with a glass slide that Phil had drawn a thick straight line on. As Cliff dropped the slide into the "image dissector," the line appeared on the small receiver in the other room. As Cliff rotated the slide, the transmitted line also turned. While the image was still very small and crude, the modern age of television was born. (The world would never be the same again.)

Every great invention seems to be noted for the first words its inventor utters when that darn thing initially works. Edison supposedly recorded "Mary had a little lamb whose fleece was white as snow. . . ." on his first phonograph recording. Bell has been quoted as saying, "Mr. Watson, come here. I need you." Let's just say that Phil Farnsworth's words were not quite as dramatic. He simply said, "There you are: electronic television."

Work continued for the next year on refining the system. The investors were looking for a return on their money, but that was still many years away. A group of the investors gathered at the Farnsworth lab in May 1928 to see their first demonstration. Farnsworth knew exactly what image he could impress these guys with. He transmitted a big dollar sign for their entertainment. They were impressed and immediately wanted to sell the whole thing, including Farnsworth and his lab gang, off to a big company that could afford to make this dream a reality. Farnsworth convinced the investors that his patent portfolio was so valuable that in the long run, they would be rewarded with much more money than they would get by cashing their chips in at that time. They decided to hang in there, at least for a while.

Word of Farnsworth's success quickly spread around the country. Hollywood actors, probably a bit concerned that they were about to be put out of work, flocked to see this newfangled device. Word eventually reached the ears of David Sarnoff, who headed the RCA behemoth. At the time, RCA controlled the world of radio. It basically owned everything related to the transmission of sound. That included all of the important patents, the transmitters, the studios, and even the license for any other company to build a radio. Dealing with RCA at the time was a do-or-die situation. You did what they said, or they would put you out of business.

It would probably come as no surprise to you that Sarnoff was worried about the effect Farnsworth and his television would have on RCA's radio monopoly. Sarnoff knew that his company had to do whatever it took to keep its existing technology from becoming obsolete.

In 1930, Sarnoff took his first step toward squashing Farnsworth. He hired a man named Vladimir K. Zworykin, a Russian émigré who was employed by Westinghouse at the time. Remember how I said that Farnsworth was not the only one in the world thinking about electronic television? You see, in 1923, Zworykin had applied for a U.S. patent for just such an invention. Unfortunately, Westinghouse had little interest in the project and it was dropped. The patent was not issued at the time, but the application remained on file.

Before having Zworykin come to RCA, Sarnoff directed him to make a visit to Farnsworth's lab in California to see what was going on. Zworykin was not to mention that he was working for RCA. When Zworykin showed up at the lab, Farnsworth was a bit too naive and explained how the whole system worked. Zworykin was amazed by what he saw and after three days of prowling around the lab, he left.

Sarnoff then took a visit out to the Farnsworth facility to see for himself what was going on. He offered Everson $100,000 for the whole kit and caboodle, including Farnsworth. Everson turned him down and Sarnoff left. But this would not be the last that would be heard from Sarnoff and the RCA monster. Sarnoff was going to control television. There were no ifs, ands, or buts about it.

In the spring of 1931, Farnsworth entered into his first licensing deal with the Philco Radio Corporation. As part of the agreement, Farnsworth had to move the entire operation east to Philadelphia, but he found out quickly that he could not function under the corporate system and quit. Additional capital was raised (a tough thing to do during the Great Depression) and Farnsworth Television was established in Philadelphia.

By 1934, Zworykin and his team at RCA had put together their own electronic television system, using much of the same technology that Zworykin had observed while visiting Farnsworth several years prior. Their new camera tube was called the Iconoscope and was nearly identical to Farnsworth's image dissector.

Hey! They can't do that. That's theft.

Well, they did. And to top that, the RCA legal team turned around and sued Farnsworth for patent interference. Their claim was very simple. Farnsworth's television system was based on Zworykin's original 1923 patent application while Zworykin was still at Westinghouse. Sarnoff knew that if he couldn't buy Farnsworth's system, he would just sue the pants off the company until it was either forced to sell to RCA or put out of business. It was the classic case of David versus Goliath.

When they got to court, RCA's major argument was that there was absolutely no way that a young kid could develop such a complicated system while still in high school. But Farnsworth had one ace up his sleeve. Remember Justin Tolman, Philo's high school chemistry teacher? He was able to reproduce in detail what young Philo had sketched on his blackboard on that fateful day in the early 1920s.

In April 1934, the U.S. Patent and Trademark Office gave its ruling on the case of *Zworykin* v. *Farnsworth*. The last sentence of the decision sums up the whole thing: "Priority of invention is awarded Philo T. Farnsworth."

In plain English, the decision came down to this. There are basically two parts to a television system. The first part captures the image and converts it to an electrical signal. On the other end is your television, which takes that electrical signal and converts it back to an image. Making the television receiver was the easy part and had been figured out many years before. Building a device that electronically captured an image was the difficult part and had eluded even the best researchers, including Zworykin. The decision made it clear that Farnsworth was the true inventor of such a device. Yes, Farnsworth was legally declared the true inventor of television.

RCA had lost. The little guy had finally won. At least it seemed that way.

Of course, RCA was not about to give up that easily. It filed an appeal and kept Farnsworth in court for years. The head honchos at RCA did everything possible to drain Farnsworth's meager resources. They knew that as long as they kept the patents in litigation, Farnsworth would be unable to license out television to any other company and earn some much-needed cash.

In the summer of 1934, it looked like the tide was about to turn for Farnsworth. He was invited to demonstrate his television system at the Franklin Institute of Philadelphia. The crowds lined up for blocks just to get a peek at television for the first time. The event was scheduled to run for ten days but proved so popular, it was extended to three weeks.

But money was still a big problem for Farnsworth. Having a successful public demonstration is great, but it doesn't help fund research. While the courts forbade him from licensing the technology to any U.S. firm, he found his savior in John Logie Baird, the guy running that mechanical system over in Great Britain. When it became clear that electronic television was the wave of the future, Baird was forced by his financial backers to negotiate a deal with Farnsworth. In exchange for $50,000, Baird now had a contract to produce electronic television in England. Much of Farnsworth's earnings went to paying off the debt accrued by fighting RCA in court.

Farnsworth had wanted to use some of this newfound capital to build a television studio, but his investors objected. So, Farnsworth built it himself. The FCC granted Farnsworth an experimental license to broadcast as W3XPF. There was one problem with these initial broadcasts. One of the peculiarities of the image dissector was that red, which should have photographed black, was broadcast as white. Blue looked almost as weird. In other words, people looked very strange. Max Factor, the man, provided the solution. Blue makeup was applied to the lips and around the eyes of the actors. They must have looked really strange in person, but they looked just fine on the tube.

The court battles with RCA continued, but Farnsworth Television pressed on. In 1937, RCA felt that it finally had the weapon to knock Farnsworth out of the race. RCA engineers had developed a new device called the image orthicon that its lawyers were sure did not violate any of Farnsworth's patents. RCA was now going to own television, and a date was set for its introduction. That was to be at the New York World's Fair in April 1939.

Sarnoff's joy did not last long. When the patent application was filed, it was soon learned that Farnsworth had been issued a patent in 1933 for a device that utilized the same technical principles. RCA was beaten again.

The world's fair came and RCA spent an incredible amount of dough promoting *its* invention. Sarnoff made sure that Zworykin and the RCA team of engineers took full credit for the invention of television, a myth that still exists to this day. (Check your favorite encyclopedia to see what it says. . . .) Of course, RCA did not own the critical patents on the invention, but that wasn't going to stop it from promoting it as its own.

That December, RCA was finally forced to admit defeat. It entered into an agreement with Farnsworth Television to pay for the use of the technology of television. Farnsworth looked like he was about to get filthy rich, but luck was once again not on his side. His battle with RCA may have been over, but another battle was brewing overseas: World War II. Once the United States entered the war, all further development of television was placed on hold. The electronics industry had to use its resources to produce radar and other military communications equipment.

Farnsworth now had a bigger problem on his hands. After such a lengthy battle with RCA, he knew that his key patents would expire by the time the war was over. And they did. When the war ended, Farnsworth pulled himself out of the day-to-day operations of the business. He became very depressed and turned to alcohol for comfort. While Farnsworth Television did eventually manufacture televisions, mismanagement placed the company in financial ruin and forced it to sell off to International Telephone and Telegraph (ITT) in 1949. Farnsworth Television was no more. Due in large part to the propaganda put out by RCA, Farnsworth's association with television would be quickly forgotten. RCA may not have beaten Farnsworth's patents, but it surely beat Farnsworth.

In 1957, Farnsworth appeared as Dr. X on the television show *I've Got a Secret*. Bill Cullen asked him, "Is this some kind of a machine that might be painful when it's used?" Dr. X responded, "Yes. Sometimes it's most painful." No one was able to guess what Farnsworth's contribution was, and he was awarded the standard prize of eighty bucks and a carton of Winston cigarettes. What a reward. None of those guys would even have had a job without Farnsworth's genius.

While Farnsworth would never have anything to do with television again, he did continue with his research. He invented the first simple electron microscope and worked on the fundamentals of radar. His greatest passion, however, was nuclear fusion. He spent the last twenty years of his life pursuing a clean, unlimited source of energy for mankind. When Farnsworth died on March 11, 1971, his name had clearly faded into obscurity. Yet his contribution continues to live on.

And to think that it all started with a field of potatoes.

Useless? Useful? I'll leave that for you to decide.

# reginald fessenden

## the world's first radio broadcaster

My dad has jokingly said over the years that there are two rules to owning a car. The first is that you live from car payment to car payment. When you make the last one, you die. His second rule is that if you hear a strange noise anywhere in your car, just turn the radio up louder and the problem will be solved.

To me, the radio is basically a mood machine. If you hear a good song come over the airwaves, crank the volume way up. If you're feeling sad, find a country station. If you're worried about the afternoon commute home, flip over to the all-news station. One quick flick of the wrist, and your mood will instantly change.

Guglielmo Marconi is the name that is constantly pounded into our heads as the inventor of modern radio. But that all depends on what you consider to be radio. If radio is the transmission of an electromagnetic frequency from a transmitter to a receiver, then Nikola Tesla gets the credit. If radio is defined as the transmission of Morse code, then Marconi certainly gets the nod.

But, in my mind, radio is the transmission of sound, be it voice or music (or what some people try to pass off as music . . .). Going totally against everything that we were ever taught in school, it turns out that Marconi was not the first person to ever transmit the human voice. It was actually done by a genius named Reginald Fessenden.

Right now you are probably saying something like, "Reginald . . . Who?!" So let me fill you in.

Reginald Aubrey Fessenden was born on October 6, 1866, in East Bolton, Quebec. In 1884, he accepted a mathematics mastership at Bishop's College but never finished his degree because of an increasing interest in the physical sciences. He left the school and accepted a position as both the headmaster and only teacher of a small private school in Bermuda. During his two years teaching in the tropical paradise, he fell in love with Helen Trott, whom he would later marry in 1890.

After his stint as a headmaster, he picked up and went to New York City in an effort to secure a job working for Thomas Edison. Initially, he was unsuccessful, but in 1885, he was given the job of assistant tester at the Edison Machine Works, which was in the process of laying electrical cables under the streets of New York. When the project was completed, he went to work in Edison's laboratory, where his hard work and high level of intelligence did not go unnoticed. While Fessenden would probably be considered a physicist today, Edison assigned him to the chemistry division. Fessenden was given the task of finding a new, inexpensive, flameproof insulating material for all of those cables that were needed to electrify the world. The incredible world of plastics was still a few years away, so it is not clear how much success Fessenden had. He was then promoted to head chemist, but when Edison ran into severe financial troubles in 1890, Fessenden found himself without a job.

Fessenden moved on to a Westinghouse subsidiary in Newark, New Jersey, where he perfected a new method of sealing incandescent bulbs. Then it was off to the Stanley Company in Pittsfield, Massachusetts, which sent Fessenden to England to learn everything that he could about electrical generation. Fessenden and his wife returned to the United States just as a severe depression broke out. He once again found himself unemployed and never received any reimbursement for the expenses associated with his trip to Europe.

In 1892, Fessenden accepted a position as a professor of electrical engineering at Purdue University, but he didn't stay long. With the backing of George Westinghouse, he took a better job at the Western University of Pennsylvania, which eventually became the

University of Pittsburgh. (Keep in mind that he didn't even have a college degree! Boy, have times changed. . . .)

During his time as a professor, Fessenden's mind was in high gear as he cranked out ingenious invention after ingenious invention. He needed a way to compactly store all of his papers, so he devised an early form of microfilm. Fessenden also designed an early solar storage battery and continued his lightbulb research for Westinghouse.

Most experts, including Marconi, subscribed to the idea that radio waves were discontinuous, an "on-off" type of transmission known as the "whiplash" effect. While Marconi's system was adequate for transmitting Morse code signals, it was incapable of transmitting voice or music. Fessenden was convinced that radio had technologically taken a wrong turn and set out to devise a system that used continuous wave transmission.

The year 1900 saw Fessenden leaving his professorship for a position with the U.S. Weather Bureau, which asked him to develop a wireless system to distribute meteorological information. Fessenden and his team were stationed on Cobb Island in Maryland, which lies in the middle of the Potomac River, approximately sixty miles southeast of Washington, D.C. Within one year, Fessenden and his team were successfully transmitting Morse code signals to an Arlington, Virginia, station about fifty miles away.

"One-two-three-four. Is it snowing where you are, Mr. Thiessen?" On December 23, 1900, Reginald Fessenden spoke those words, the first ever broadcast through thin air. Mr. Thiessen, about one mile away, acknowledged by Morse code that he had, in fact, clearly heard what Fessenden said. As revolutionary as this may seem today, the world was basically uninterested at the time. No one saw any commercial value to transmitting the human voice, so this was perceived as nothing more than a novelty. Marconi achieved much greater accolades when he received his first transatlantic transmission of the letter *s* via Morse code one year later.

Fessenden knew that his system was crude and constantly worked on producing stronger, clearer radio transmissions. While public interest was minimal, word spread to various U.S. and Mexican governmental agencies about his invention, and orders began to come in. Willis Moore, then chief of the U.S. Weather Bureau, became aware of this increasing interest and demanded a cut of Fessenden's earnings. Luckily for Fessenden, his contract allowed him to retain his patents, and he left the job in 1902.

With the financial backing of two millionaires, Thomas H. Given and Hay Walker, the National Electric Signalling Company (NESCO) was founded. Since there was so little interest at the time in what was called telephony, the company focused its attention on improved telegraphy. It set up several stations along the northeastern coast of the United States. The company's first real success was on January 10, 1906, when Fessenden and his team made the first successful two-way transatlantic transmission between Brant Rock, Massachusetts, and Scotland. Once again, there was little interest in their product. Customers just didn't see the need for the best and most expensive equipment to transmit Morse code. They opted for similar, less expensive equipment from other manufacturers.

Fessenden continued to work on the equipment to transmit voice. He correctly concluded that high-frequency signals were the key to clarifying transmissions, and demonstrated the revolutionary heterodyne theory. While others later improved upon it, this principle is still fundamental to radio today. The concept is a bit technical, but without it, you would need a separate receiver for each radio channel.

One of NESCO's customers was the United Fruit Company, whose ships were outfitted with NESCO's wireless equipment. Fessenden told United Fruit's wireless operators to listen for "something different" on Christmas Eve of 1906. At 9 P.M., strange sounds were heard coming out of their receivers. It was the human voice! Fessenden said a few words and then played Handel's "Largo" on the Ediphone (making him the world's first deejay) and then followed by playing "O Holy Night" on his violin and singing the last verse himself. Just imagine the thrill of hearing the first radio program of all time. It must have been simply amazing.

Fessenden's broadcast was heard as far away as the West Indies, and at his request, listeners mailed in letters confirming that they had witnessed history in the making. Sadly, this would be the high point of Fessenden's radio career.

Marconi once again stole Fessenden's thunder by establishing transatlantic wireless telegraph service on a regular basis. Then, to top that, Marconi was granted the exclusive right to build wireless stations in Canada, effectively locking NESCO out of the market.

In 1908, NESCO attempted to oust Fessenden from the company. Fessenden was considered nothing more than an obstacle to the company's profitability. It had control of his patents and no longer needed him. As you would expect, this whole mess ended up in court, a battle that would last nearly the remainder of Fessenden's life.

While this marked the end of Fessenden's involvement with radio development, he continued to use his inventive mind. Between 1911 and 1912, he developed a turboelectric drive for battleships. In 1912, he devised an array of equipment that allowed submarines to send and receive signals. As a result of the *Titanic* disaster, Fessenden modified some of his equipment to detect icebergs miles away. His creation of an early form of television known as the pheroscope, the designs of an electric gyroscope and a lightweight automobile engine, and the idea to place phosphorus on machine-gun bullets as a tracer only add to his long list of lifetime achievements.

Financially, his 1921 creation of the Fathometer, used as a depth finder for ships and submarines, may have been his most rewarding. The sale of this invention for $50,000 to the Submarine Signalling Company finally gave him the financial security that he had long sought.

While Fessenden created all of these fantastic inventions, he continued his legal fight against NESCO. By this time, his patents were in the hands of RCA. His legal troubles continued until March 31, 1928, when the case was settled out of court. RCA was reported to have paid Fessenden half a million dollars for patent infringement.

Fessenden and his wife purchased waterfront property in

Bermuda, where he remained until his death from heart failure on July 22, 1932. With hundreds of patents to his name, the father of radio died largely forgotten. Perhaps you can start spreading the word about what a remarkable man Reginald Fessenden was and help correct the terrible injustice with which history has rewarded his creativity.

Useless? Useful? I'll leave that for you to decide.

# photographic film

## eastman kodak's big loss

I have always had a keen interest in old technology. Scattered around my place are basically worthless old cameras, radios, and other obsolete gadgets. My favorite is a 1930 Bell & Howell movie projector that my grandparents gave to me several years ago. Because it is still in perfect running condition, I can't help but stare at it and wonder what it must have been like to see moving images preserved on celluloid for the first time.

The majority of the earliest photographs, as you probably already know, were taken on glass plates, which were extremely fragile, bulky, and very expensive. Early photographers eagerly sought out a substitute for the glass plate, but nothing available at the time seemed to fit the bill. The specifications for this new material were quite broad: lightweight, flexible, transparent, strong, and, most of all, capable of producing pictures of high quality.

The real key to solving the flexible film problem lay in the newly discovered world of plastics. The first true plastic was Alexander Parkes's invention, appropriately called Parkesine. It was a commercial failure, but Parkes was the first to attempt to manufacture a plastic film for photography. His film was derived from collodion, which was basically a dried varnish whose main ingredients were nitrated cotton (guncotton) and some solvents to liquefy it.

Parkes may have set the foundation for flexible film, but it was the discovery of celluloid by John Wesley Hyatt that really set the wheels of technology into motion. Celluloid differed little chemically from Parkesine, but Hyatt's addition of camphor allowed the plastic to be reheated and remolded over and over again. Oddly, Hyatt and his brother Isaiah were not in search of a new photographic medium. With natural ivory in short supply at the time, they had intended their product to be used to make billiard balls.

As celluloid products became more commonplace, photographers were convinced that it might be the material that they had been searching for. John Carbutt of Philadelphia started experimenting with celluloid plates in 1884 and began selling them commercially in 1888. These new photographic plates were made by shaving off thin slices from blocks of compressed celluloid. Other manufacturers soon followed with similar celluloid-based products, but they all failed to catch on with photographers. First, the images produced were inferior to those produced on glass. Additionally, the film was a bit too thick to be considered flexible.

Which leads us to the next character in our story. . . .

In June 1888, George Eastman marketed the first Kodak camera. His camera did not use glass or celluloid plates. Instead, inside each camera was a reel of paper coated with a photosensitive emulsion. After shooting the 100-snapshot roll, the consumer simply mailed it back to Eastman for developing. The pictures were developed at the plant, and the camera was reloaded with film and returned to the consumer. While this introduced photography to the masses, the process of removing the emulsion from the paper was incredibly delicate and inefficient, and produced images of poor quality.

Like other photographers, Eastman was keenly aware that celluloid and its collodion derivatives might be the Holy Grail of photography that he had been seeking. Eastman did a number of experiments with the collodion varnishes but did not have any success. Eastman needed someone with a greater understanding of chemistry and soon hired Henry Reichenbach, then a chemistry graduate student at the University of Rochester. Although the two men worked closely on the project, it was Reichenbach that finally found just the right concoction that produced the perfect film.

You can be sure that the dollar signs were flashing in their eyes. $$$!!! $$$!!! $$$!!!

They rushed their patent application to the U.S. Patent and Trademark Office. There was a brief delay for an interference proceeding regarding a similar patent application, but the patent examiner concluded that Reichenbach's application was unique and issued the patent on December 10, 1889. As expected, Eastman Kodak made millions and millions on the process.

But wait! That is not the end of the story. . . .

That similar patent application mentioned above belonged to Hannibal Goodwin, an elderly Episcopalian minister from Newark, New Jersey. Lantern slides were all the rage in the late 1870s, but Goodwin was unable to find suitable biblical pictures. There were plenty of pictures of Niagara Falls, Yellowstone, and the like, but there were none of Bethlehem and Jerusalem to be found anywhere. He decided to start making his own slides but quickly discovered what photographers of his day knew all too well: Glass-plate photography was a royal pain in the you-know-what.

Goodwin knew that there had to be a better way and naively set upon trying to find a substitute for glass plates. He had no scientific education and basically little understanding of chemistry, yet after about a year of toiling in the attic of his rectory, he discovered a formula that truly did work. On May 2, 1887, Goodwin submitted his application for "Photographic Pellicle and Process of Producing Same" to the patent office. It was firmly rejected. He made revision after revision, but each time, the application was returned to him for further clarification. Basically, Goodwin's claims were too broad, his chemical explanations were imprecise, and the patent as a whole was poorly worded.

When Reichenbach's patent was issued nearly two years later, Goodwin was stunned. He was certain that his invention was nearly identical. Again, Goodwin's patent application was revised, resubmitted, and rejected over and over again. Finally, on January 18, 1892, the patent office decided to reopen the interference proceeding between the Goodwin and Reichenbach claims.

Initially, it was concluded that the Reichenbach patent was valid because the formula contained large amounts of camphor. (Keep in mind that camphor was celluloid's magic ingredient.) Goodwin's did not contain any camphor and, as a result, the burden of proof fell on Goodwin's shoulders. Going up against a big, powerful corporation was expensive, and it was clear that this was a battle that Goodwin was not going to win. His pockets were just not deep enough.

But the tide was about to change for Goodwin. He couldn't fight against the powerful Eastman Kodak lawyers, but another powerful company could. The Celluloid Manufacturing Company felt that Reichenbach's patent infringed on its patents and took Kodak to court. Kodak was forced to change its recipe by reducing the amount of camphor in the formula. This ended up being beneficial to Kodak, since the removal of camphor decreased the drying time and increased the rate of production.

You can see where this is going. By removing the camphor from the mix to avoid a fight with Celluloid, the formula for Eastman Kodak film was dangerously close to that of Goodwin.

While this was all going on at Eastman Kodak, Goodwin finally received his patent for the camphorless flexible film formula on September 13, 1898, more than eleven years after he first filed his application. Goodwin was now seventy-six years old, but he was still willing to fight for his share of the pie. He founded the Goodwin Film & Camera Company in Newark, while his investors and legal team explored the possibility of taking on the film giant Eastman Kodak in court. Yet, victory over Eastman Kodak was not something that Goodwin would live to see. He died in a street accident near a construction site on December 31, 1900. Seven months later, his wife sold the Goodwin patents to the Anthony and Scovill companies, which later merged into Ansco, a large New York photographic-supply house. Frederick Anthony tried to avoid taking Eastman to court and offered him the patent for a half a million dollars in cash and another half a million in Eastman Kodak stock. Eastman refused and, instead, welcomed the onslaught of Ansco's lawyers. Ansco filed suit in 1902 and battled it out in court until March 1914, when a final appeals-court ruling found in favor of Goodwin. After twenty-seven years of patent revisions and court fights, Goodwin was declared the original inventor of flexible photographic film.

The rectory of the House of Prayer in Newark, New Jersey. Built around 1710, it is considered to be the oldest dwelling in the city. It was in this building that the Reverend Hannibal Goodwin invented celluloid photographic film. (Library of Congress)

Eastman Kodak dished out $5 million for the patent infringement, which was reported to have been approximately 5 percent of George Eastman's fortune at the time. A portion of the settlement was turned over to the Goodwin estate, but that is not the end of the story. As you are probably well aware, any time that someone stumbles across a big wad of cash, the lawyers come running. A suit relating to a reorganization of the company's finances back in 1903 was filed against Ansco by a group of its investors. The Goodwin estate was sued by the family of a man that was supposedly Goodwin's partner and played a key role in the invention of the film. These things have a way of being quietly settled, however, and in the end, Goodwin's name stood out as the first inventor of flexible photographic film.

Useless? Useful? I will leave that for you to decide.

# the photocopier

## the invention that nobody wanted

May 6, 1997.

What's so significant about this date?

Not much.

It just happens to be the date that I was in my school's copy room fixing our high-speed photocopier. I somehow ended up being the resident copier-repair guy. It typically boils down to this: If I can't fix it, it's time to call the service guy.

So there I was kneeling on the floor pulling the jammed sheets of paper out of the machine, when I took a quick glance down at the counter. It was at about 1.3 million copies. Surely I read it wrong. This machine was fewer than four years old; that count seemed unrealistic. So I looked down again and this time counted the number of digits to make sure it really was in the million range. It certainly was.

It then occurred to me how important this machine was. Our school's staff had reproduced 1.3 million pages of educational material for approximately 400 students in just four short years.

We're all guilty of wasting a tree or two to make photocopies. Just push a button and a copy comes out the other end (assuming the machine doesn't eat the paper for lunch). It couldn't be much simpler.

But it wasn't always that simple. The basic process that we take for granted today took a lot of blood, sweat, and tears to develop.

Yet, when the photocopier methodology was finally realized, nobody wanted it. Nobody except its inventor, Chester F. Carlson.

Little Chester was born way back on February 8, 1906, in that great city of Seattle. His father was an itinerant barber who ended up settling the family in San Bernardino, California. Unfortunately, his father developed crippling arthritis. Then, to make things even worse, both Mom and Dad contracted tuberculosis. By the time Chester was fourteen years old, he was the main source of income for the Carlson household. Mom died when Chester was seventeen years old.

Yet, despite all of Chester's hardships, he managed to enroll himself in a junior college in Riverside, California. He then moved on to earn his bachelor of science degree in physics from the California Institute of Technology in 1930. This left him $1,400 in the hole during the depression. Finding a job to pay off this debt was not easy. Chester sent out letters to eighty-two different companies. He received only two replies, and no job offers.

Chester ended up working as a research engineer for Bell Labs in New York City for just $35 a week. This job didn't last very long. As the depression deepened, Bell was forced to lay Chester off.

Realizing that he probably could not find a job in his desired field, Chester settled for a job at the electronics firm of P. R. Mallory, which was famous for its dry-cell batteries. He was eventually promoted to manager of Mallory's patent department. At night, he went to law school to become a patent lawyer.

This dead-end job at P. R. Mallory ended up leading Chester Carlson to the invention that would change the world. He found that there were never enough copies of patents around. There were only two choices at the time to get more copies: Either send the patents out to be photographed or laboriously write new ones. Both methods proved to be very expensive and time consuming. To make matters worse, Carlson was nearsighted and began to suffer from arthritis.

Carlson knew there had to be a better way to make copies. The only problem was that no one knew how. He was going to find out.

It would have been nice if Carlson had immediately found a solution to this copy problem, but it wasn't that easy.

His first step was to head straight to the library—the New York Public Library, to be specific. He spent many months poring over tons of scientific articles. Articles related to the field of photography were immediately ruled out. This field was loaded with corporate researchers who had extensively analyzed every nook and cranny of the process. Besides, photography could be wet and messy.

No, the answer to quick copies had to lie elsewhere.

Carlson turned his attention to the field of photoconductivity. This was a relatively new field that was discovered by the Hungarian physicist Paul Selenyi. It seems that when light strikes the surface of certain materials, its conductivity (flow of electrons) increases.

Carlson, being a physicist, had that flash of inspiration that all inventors talk so much about. Perhaps you just made the same realization. (You're about fifty years too late.) Carlson realized that if the image of an original photograph or document were projected onto a photoconductive surface, current would flow only in the areas that light hit. The print areas would be dark and not allow any current to flow.

But, as all inventors know, inspiration doesn't make for an invention—it's the perspiration. You know, thirty seconds to think of the solution, sometimes an entire lifetime to actually get it to work.

Carlson set up his lab in every inventor's favorite workplace: the kitchen. It was in the kitchen of his Jackson Heights, Queens, apartment that the basic principles of what he termed "electrophotography" were formed. He applied for his first patent in October 1937.

Unfortunately, Carlson's wife was getting sick of his endless experiments and demanded that he get out of her kitchen. (She eventually walked out of his life for good. I bet she regretted that decision after he made his millions.) The laboratory was moved to a room in the back of a beauty salon in Astoria, Queens, owned by his mother-in-law. Since he was suffering from arthritis and had little patience for the endless experiments, Chester hired an unemployed German physicist named Otto Kornei to help him out.

You may recall from your high school earth science classes that sulfur is a yellow mineral that does not conduct electricity. This is true, but when exposed to light, it will conduct a small amount of charge. So, one day Otto took a zinc plate and coated it with a freshly prepared batch of sulfur. He then wrote the words *10-22-38 Astoria* on a microscope slide in India ink. The room was darkened. The sulfur was rubbed with a handkerchief to give it a charge. The slide was then placed on top of the sulfur and placed under a bright light for a few seconds. The slide was then removed and the sulfur surface was covered with lycopodium powder (the waxy spores from club moss).

Drum roll, please . . .

With one giant breath of air, the lycopodium was blown off the sulfur surface. And there it was, an almost exact mirror image that said—you guessed it—"10-22-38 Astoria."

The real trick was in preserving the image. Carlson took waxed paper and heated it over the remaining powder. The paper cooled around the spores and was then peeled away. Yes, the first photocopy (if you consider the spores of a fungus to be a copy) had been made.

Needless to say, this product was not quite ready for the office. A tremendous amount of work still needed to be done, but Carlson's theory was confirmed. But, research takes money, and Carlson didn't have any. Kornei couldn't see where this was all leading and quit. He went to work for IBM and was later rewarded for his efforts with stock from Carlson.

With such a great product, one would think that companies would be banging at Carlson's door throwing large wads of cash into his lap. This was not the case. Between 1939 and 1944, Carlson was turned down by more than twenty of the large corporations, including IBM, Kodak, General Electric, and RCA.

During this time, Carlson's continued work at P. R. Mallory occasionally took him to the Battelle Memorial Institute, a nonprofit organization in Columbus, Ohio, that invested in technological research. During one visit in 1944, Carlson casually mentioned that he held several patents on a new reproduction process. As a result of this encounter, Battelle officials expressed interest and signed a royalty-sharing deal with Carlson, giving Carlson a 40 percent share in the proceeds. Battelle was well aware of the amount of research that needed to be done but went to work to solve the many problems.

Battelle assigned the project to a man named Roland M. Schaffert, a research physicist and a former printer. Schaffert worked on the project all by his lonesome for nearly a year. (After all, this was during World War II, and our nation's research energy was focused elsewhere.) When the war ended, Battelle provided Schaffert with a small group of assistants to improve on the process.

The first step that the Battelle team took was to develop a new photoconductive plate. Carlson's sulfur plate just didn't do it. Instead, Battelle developed a new plate that was covered with selenium, which was a much better photoconductor. Next, it spent nearly a year developing the corona wire to serve a dual role: to apply the electrostatic charge to the plate and to transfer the powder from the plate to the paper.

One of the most important developments was the invention of a better dry ink. Carlson's use of lycopodium powder and other materials produced a somewhat blurry image. Battelle researchers substituted a fine iron powder for dry ink and mixed in ammonium chloride salt and a plastic material. The ammonium chloride was included to clean up the image. It had the same charge as the metal plate, so in the areas where there was low charge or no image, the iron particles stuck to the salt and not to the plate. The plastic material was designed to melt when heated and fused the iron particles to the paper. They called this material "toner," since one could very simply use different tones of developer to produce any color desired. (Three superimposed colors could be used to produce full-color copies.)

On January 2, 1947, Battelle signed a licensing agreement with a small Rochester company known as Haloid. Haloid manufactured photographic products at the time and was looking for new technology to develop. Haloid's investment in electrophotography was a big gamble, since the company had only earned $101,000 on sales of $6,750,000 in 1946. The research would cost Haloid a minimum investment of $25,000 a year.

Battelle and Haloid demonstrated electrophotography to the world on October 22, 1948, ten years to the day after Carlson's first successful experiment. The first photocopiers were introduced in 1949. The whole process was inefficient and was not practical when making a dozen or more copies. It took fourteen different steps by the user and some forty-five seconds to produce a single copy. These flat-plate (as opposed to the rotating drums currently used) machines were rejected for being too complicated.

Back to the drawing board.

At the same time, Haloid came up with a better name for the process. Somehow the term *electrophotography* was not very catchy. An Ohio State professor suggested *xerography*, from the Greek words *xeros* for "dry" and *graphos* for "writing." Haloid named its first photocopier the XeroX Model A, the last *X* being added to make the name similar to that of Kodak, another Rochester corporation. In 1958, Haloid officially changed its name to Haloid Xerox, and finally to just plain old Xerox in 1961.

Success didn't really come to Haloid until 1959, when it introduced the Model 914, the first fully automated photocopier. It was called the 914 because it could handle paper up to nine by fourteen inches in size (legal size). This machine was so popular that by the end of 1961, Xerox had nearly $60 million in revenue. By 1965, revenues leaped to over $500 million.

Of course, all good things must come to an end. Chester Carlson, finally enjoying the profits from his years of hard work, collapsed and died on September 19, 1968, while walking down Fifty-seventh Street in New York City. He had been attending a conference and was on his way to see a movie during some spare time. Of the estimated $150 million he had earned from Xerox, he had generously given about $100 million to charity.

A very nice deed on the part of the man who changed our lives forever. And to think that nobody wanted his invention.

Useless? Useful? I'll leave that for you to decide.

## PART 3

# hard to believe

# neil armstrong

## was he really the first to walk on the moon?

When you think of the moon, you almost certainly envision a barren, rocky wasteland, an inhospitable place with no atmosphere, no running water, and no living organisms. Yet, back in the summer of 1835, the people of the United States were under a much different impression of the moon. Published reports, based on the findings of one of the world's leading astronomers, surely pointed toward the inevitable conclusion that the moon was a paradise.

**Tuesday, August 25, 1835**

The change in people's view of the moon started on this morning with the *New York Sun*'s story simply titled "Great Astronomical Discoveries Lately Made by Sir John Herschel." The story, written by Dr. Andrew Grant, Herschel's assistant, was from a soon-to-be-published supplement to the *Edinburgh Journal of Science*. Herschel, whose father had discovered the planet Uranus (one name you should never, ever, mention in a high school classroom!), had traveled to South Africa to map out the largely uncharted southern view of the universe. The article described in great detail a new telescope that Herschel had designed, one that was so large and revolutionary that it was capable of seeing objects in greater detail than had ever been seen before. The entire article was filled with all types of technical jargon, including some historical information on Herschel and the specifics of his new scope. Yet, it only hinted at the great things that Herschel had actually discovered. That was left for another day with the simple words "To be continued."

## Wednesday, August 26, 1835

Wednesday's installment started out just like the previous day's story, with lots of scientific jibber-jabber that no one really cared about. Then, about ten long paragraphs into the story, there appeared the sub-heading "New Lunar Discoveries." Read it too fast, and you would have missed the most important line! After a brief description of the lunar surface were the simple words "covered with a dark red flower."

Yes, you read it correctly. Herschel, with the aid of his mighty telescope, had apparently discovered the "first organic production of nature, in a foreign world, ever revealed to the eyes of men." (And we are still looking for it!) Herschel went on to conclude that the moon had an "atmosphere constituted similarly to our own" and could possibly sustain animal life.

The article then moved on to describe a few other types of vegetation observed but then quickly changed its focus to describing the surface of the moon. The discovery of giant amethyst crystals, some as tall as ninety feet, was detailed.

Then there was the revelation that animal life had been observed on the moon. First there were the herds of brown quadrupeds having the "characteristics of the bison" but much smaller. This was then followed by details of another animal that was described as bluish lead in color, approximately the size of a goat, and having just one horn. (Can we say . . . unicorn?)

I am sure that you are buying all this, huh? Well, it appears that the readers of the day certainly did, whether they actually believed it all or not. Circulation of the *Sun* increased dramatically. To make sure that readers were hooked, the article was finished with a teaser, "Further animal discoveries were made of the most exciting interest to every human being."

What were these discoveries? That's where those wonderful words that we all hate came into play: "To be continued."

## Thursday, August 27, 1835

Starting with more details that the average person could not care less about, this day's entry discussed the discovery of giant mountain chains, erupting volcanoes, and even water.

Herschel then went on to classify a large bunch of newly dis-covered plants and animals. For example, there were nine species of mammals, including small reindeer, moose, elk, miniature zebras, *horned* bears, and biped beavers. The beaver was the most interest-ing because it walked "upon only two feet," carried "its young in its arms like a human being," used fire, and lived in a well-constructed hut.

Just what was Herschel smoking here?

You know what words came next.

"To be continued."

**Friday, August 28, 1835**

After the discoveries recounted on the previous day, surely there was little left to discover on the moon. Well, think again!

This day's article now reported the finding of flocks of large winged creatures that were "wholly unlike any kind of birds" and were incredibly graceful in flight. They were human in form and were capable of walking in an upright position. (I believe that we call these things angels down here on planet Earth.)

The typical winged creature was just four feet high and was cov-ered with "glossy copper-colored hair," except on the face. Its wings were capable of "great expansion" and were "similar in structure to this of the bat." The creatures were conferred with the scientific name *Vespertilio homo,* which means "bat man" in plain English.

What more wonderful discoveries would they find on the moon?

"To be continued."

**Saturday, August 29, 1835**

On this day, three giant oceans and numerous seas and lakes were described. But that's just boring stuff. Clearly, any batman (get it?) must have an organized religion. The article went on to describe in great detail a newly discovered temple on the moon. It was built from "polished sapphire" and was so large that it could not fit within the viewing area of the telescope. Nothing like this had ever been seen before on earth. (As exciting as this discovery was, this article was a letdown from the previous day's.)

"To be continued."

**Monday, August 31, 1835**

(Clearly, they needed a day of rest from all of the excitement, so they took Sunday off.)

This day's article was largely devoted to the habits of the batman. "They spent their happy hours in collecting fruits in the woods, in eating, flying, bathing, and loitering about on the summits of precipices." The article pointed out that these individuals "were of larger stature than the former specimens, less dark in color, and in every respect an improved variety of the race." (Sounds a bit prejudiced here . . .)

Then the really bad news came.

In all the excitement of these great discoveries, they did not shut down the telescope properly for the night. As the sun rose the next morning, its focused beam of light set the observatory on fire and severely damaged the great telescope. It took about a week of intense labor to get it back in service, at which time the moon was no longer visible. Herschel focused his attentions once again on mapping the southern sky.

After some descriptions about some planetary observations, the series of articles was brought to a close with the words "This concludes the supplement."

**The Aftermath**

With the exclusive right to publish this incredible series of articles, the *Sun* took claim to the largest circulation of any newspaper in the world. It prepared an illustrated pamphlet and sold an estimated 60,000 copies within one month. The leading scientists and mathematicians of the day, most credible (and not-so-credible) newspapers, and the everyday Joe were all caught up in the sensation. The series was translated into many languages and the story slowly circulated its way across Europe.

The only real problem with this whole story was that it wasn't true at all. (I'm sure that you knew that from the first sentence.) Herschel, who really was in South Africa at the time studying the southern sky, had never made any of these claims. He'd made some very important discoveries but nothing so outrageous.

The big question, then, was, Who actually wrote these articles?

Was this all part of an elaborate hoax or was it based on some sort of real observations? As time passed, more and more people questioned the authenticity of the story, but with no hard evidence, it was impossible to disprove the claims that were made.

It turned out that it was all a big scheme on the part of the *Sun* to increase circulation. The articles were actually written by the paper's editor, Richard Adams Locke. At a time when newspapers both reported the news and entertained, it was not uncommon for fiction to be published in serial form. Locke, as he had done in previous stories for the paper, used his great writing skills to get the public to buy papers. Yet, the moon story somehow took on a life of its own. And let's face it, when you have a cash cow, you milk it for everything that it's worth. (Just think of the $$$ earned off the likes of Marilyn Monroe, Elvis, O. J. Simpson, Princess Diana, and JonBenet Ramsey. The media coverage on all of these topics never ends.)

As the story grew in popularity, other newspapers started to publish accounts of the great discoveries. But when a competing paper, the *Journal of Commerce*, decided to actually ask the *Sun* for permission to publish the story in its entirety, Locke was finally forced to come clean. At first, he tried to dissuade the *Journal*'s editors from publishing the story on the grounds that it was basically old news. When they still expressed interest, Locke was finally forced to admit that he had created the whole thing for the *Sun*. The *Journal*, of course, revealed the scam to the whole world, but neither the *Sun* nor Locke ever publicly admitted that it was a hoax. Some readers apparently dismissed the whole thing with a chuckle, while others refused to believe that they had been conned.

Eventually, copies of the story made it into the hands of Herschel, who laughed the whole thing off. When he finally returned to England, the rest of the world must have been sorely disappointed with his meager discoveries. Yet, he went on to live a distinguished life and made significant contributions to the then new field of photography.

Useless? Useful? I'll leave that for you to decide.

# astronots

## did they really have the right stuff?

Did you know that you have been deceived, that you have fallen for the greatest hoax in the history of mankind? Just enter my class-room, and my students will quickly have you convinced that no one has ever landed on the moon. Never, ever.

Now, having been a high school science teacher for many years, I have had to deal with my share of debates and controversies. But this one takes the cake. No matter what I say in response to the stu-dents' claims that the moon landings never occurred, I am just plain wrong.

The moon landings, at least based on my students' assessment of the evidence, were filmed on a movie set in the legendary Area 51 of the Nevada desert. The U.S. government was so desperate to beat the Soviet Union in the space race that it faked all six of the Apollo moon missions.

*That's a lie,* I say. . . .

"No," my students claim. I am just one of the many billions of people tricked by the U.S. government into believing that this ficti-tious event actually happened.

*But I have proof,* I say. . . .

"No, you're wrong, Mr. Silverman. We saw it on television last night. It was on FOX and they proved that it was one big hoax. There is absolutely no evidence that anyone has ever stepped foot on that big white sphere that revolves around us."

*But I HAVE proof,* I say. . . .

It appears that my long-held belief that men have walked on the moon has been placed on trial. So, we'll let you be the judge. Let's take a look at the evidence my students have repeatedly brought up:

You are about to enter the courtroom of Judge Judith . . . (Oops, wrong scenario.)

*Student exhibit A:* "Take a look at the videos of men erecting the U.S. flags on the moon. The flags are all blowing in the wind. The moon has no atmosphere. No atmosphere means no wind. No wind means the flag should not move. Duh!"

*Mr. Silverman's defense:* "While the FOX network is best known for airing controversial programs like *Who Wants to Marry a Multi-Millionaire?, Temptation Island,* and *Married with Children,* we will assume for argument's sake that this was one of its highest-quality programs. Any preconceived image that you may have of FOX should be set aside. So, let's move on to your first piece of evidence: the moving flag.

"The flag was waving in the wind, huh? Give me a break. It may appear that way, but look all around the area. If the winds are blowing that fast, why is the extra-fine moon dust sitting still?

"You are correct that there is no wind on the moon. If you look at all the film footage of flags moving in the supposed wind on the moon, you will note that in each case, an astronaut is moving the pole. The fact that there is no wind should not lead you to the conclusion that the laws of physics no longer apply here. This is not much different from the idea that you would feel no pain kicking a weightless bowling ball in space! (Ouch!)

"The flag has inertia (an object in motion stays in motion) and is subject to many of the same forces found on earth, excluding wind. Move the pole, and the flag will move with it. Since gravity on the moon is one-sixth what it is down here on this third rock from the sun, the swinging motions of the flag and pole do not die out nearly as quickly as one would assume."

*Student exhibit B:* "Tons of photographs were taken on the moon. No stars can be seen anywhere. The sky is pitch black.

Common sense clearly tells us that a dark sky should clearly show all of the very bright stars. Duh!"

*Mr. Silverman's defense:* "There is a very good reason that you can't see the stars. The moon has no atmosphere to spread out the sun's light. During our daytime, the atmosphere causes the dispersion of light and our sky appears bright. On the moon, this is not the case. The sunlight comes in and reflects off everything on the surface, which makes it a very bright place to walk around when the sun has risen. The objects are bright, but the vacuum of space still appears dark. Any amateur photographer could tell you that the only way to take a photograph of a bright object would be to close the aperture of the camera way down and take a very quick picture. If too much light enters the camera, the film will be overexposed. The stars, however, are very, very far away, and little of their light makes it our way across the universe. As a result, the stars are just too dim to be exposed on the film.

"Even on earth at night, one has to keep the camera shutter open for a long period of time to capture enough light to see the stars. The fraction of a second that it took the astronauts to take each photograph was just too short. If you don't believe me, just take your camera out on a dark night and snap a picture of a bright light like a street lamp. Get the film developed and I guarantee that you will not see any stars in the image."

*Student exhibit C:* "Every rocket ever sent into space has a flaming exhaust. Yet, if you look at the video of the top half of the orbiter leaving the moon, it is clear that no flames are coming out of its exhaust. Obviously, they never took off from the moon. Duh!"

*Mr. Silverman's defense:* "Yes, every rocket that we send into space has a flaming exhaust. But we have oxygen down here on earth that allows fuel to burn. In space, it's a whole different story. Different chemicals are used. When they are mixed, they produce an exhaust. The exhaust, however, does not need to be a bright red or blue flame. Just think about your high school chemistry experiments. Did every chemical reaction actually result in the production of a flame? Most likely it did not, yet it probably had no problem giving off a tremendous volume of gas that stunk up the whole school building."

*Student exhibit D:* "There is that famous footage of Neil Armstrong stepping out of the lunar module blurting out the words, 'That's one small step for (a) man, one giant leap . . .' Also, there is footage of the same module blasting back into space. No one was on the moon before or after the supposed landing, so how could these photographs be real? Clearly, it was done back here on earth. Duh!"

*Mr. Silverman's defense:* "Just use your imagination here. Let's suppose you were going to land on a strange planet for the first time and knew that you had to capture that first step on film for the sake of posterity. How would you get a picture of the momentous event?

*Apollo 11* astronaunt Buzz Aldrin standing before the U.S. flag on the surface of the moon. Are the ripples in the flag proof-positive that man has never actually landed on the moon? (NASA)

The solution is actually quite simple. The camera was attached to an arm that swung out from the base of the lunar module. At the end of the mission, the LM's base with the camera still attached stayed behind to film the launch from the moon's surface."

*Student exhibit E:* "Radiation. Radiation. Radiation. The astronauts had to fly through a belt of high radiation to get to the moon. The rocket would have needed lead walls several feet thick to stop the radiation from killing the astronauts. The rockets were not made of lead and, therefore, it is impossible that anyone ever went to the moon. Duh!"

*Mr. Silverman's defense:* "It is a known fact that the astronauts had to fly through a zone of radiation, known as the Van Allen belt, to get to the moon. The amount of radiation, however, that the hoax supporters have tossed around is highly exaggerated.

"It is estimated that each astronaut was exposed to 1 rem of radiation each way, for a total of 2 rem. To place this value in perspective, the average person on earth is exposed to 0.1 to 0.2 rem of radiation each year. This radiation comes from all types of sources: the soil, rocks, cosmic rays, air, food, water, radon gas, and many other things. People who work with nuclear materials may be exposed to 5 rem a year, or as much as 25 rem in a single emergency situation, without adverse effects. The effects of radiation exposure typically do not show up until exposures of 25 rem or more have occurred.

"NASA knew that there was an unknown danger from flying through the Van Allen belt. Scientists had previously calculated that, excluding passing through during a period of intense solar flares, the astronauts would not be exposed to deadly levels of radiation. The time of exposure was relatively short, on the order of a few hours, and the astronauts made it through safely."

Let's bring this debate to a close. . . .

*Students' closing remarks:* "There is a ton more evidence that proves that man never landed on the moon. They discussed it all on the FOX program. There is absolutely no proof that man ever went to the moon. Duh!"

*Mr. Silverman's closing remarks:* "You are all too young to remember when we sent men to the moon. Because I'm an antique, one memory of the entire event stands out clearly in my mind. While it was a fascinating time in history, the actual event was just plain boring. *Boring!* Hour upon hour of basically nothing but poor photography and little action. I just can't help but wonder that if NASA really did film this historic moment on earth, couldn't it have done a lot better? Just think, it could have been the movie *Titanic* of its day—everyone glued to his or her television set to follow the love story and the tragic turn of events that would lead to heartbreak. Add to that the stunning Leonardo DiCaprio of the day and a syrupy Céline Dion type of song to accompany it.

"There is certainly nothing wrong with questioning anything. In fact, it should be highly encouraged. But balance is key to the scientific method. To just examine one side of the evidence is not the proper method of research. The fact that FOX basically presented only the viewpoint of hoax supporters should make one question the conclusions reached.

"Sure, there are some inconsistencies in the facts. A little thought, however, goes a long way in explaining these doubts away. Just keep in mind that the moon program involved tens of thousands of people, and yet not a single person has come forward to break his or her silence. Add to that the tens of thousands of people that actually witnessed the launching of the Apollo spacecrafts off the ground. The space program produced an incredible amount of documentation and left a paper trail that would be a future historian's dream come true. Let's not forget the 400 kilograms of moon rock that have been examined by hundreds of trained scientists from nations all over the world. These rocks are clearly not of earth origin and these scientists have never questioned their authenticity.

"The only real solution to this debate would be to send another person to the moon. But then, that mission would be dismissed as a hoax also. If we continue to base our opinions on one-sided journalism, we will someday have a world that believes that the earth is flat, Elvis is still walking the streets, Martians built the great pyramids, Pearl Harbor was a product of Hollywood, and the Holocaust never happened."

But then, maybe my original approach was the best one. We should just let Judge Judy decide this one.

Useless? Useful? I'll leave that for you to decide.

# mayday at 41,000 feet

## watch those units!

As a longtime science teacher, many times I get answers like this to mathematical problems: "Twelve."

Like any well-trained dog—I mean, teacher—I automatically blurt back, "Twelve *what?* Are we talking about twelve eggs, twelve pencils, twelve pounds, twelve liters, or twelve pieces of metabab-baboobinite? Twelve *what?*"

Watching for mathematical units is one of those lessons that students just never seem to want to pay attention to. Homework upon homework, test upon test, my students consistently leave the units off their work.

Now, I am sure that you are familiar with the case of NASA's Mars Climate Orbiter, which crashed into the surface of the red planet back in September 1999. Within weeks, an investigation board determined that the NASA engineers had failed to convert pounds to newtons when measuring rocket force. The monetary cost to the people of the United States and the embarrassment to NASA were hefty. Yet, no human life was ever placed in danger.

On Saturday, July 23, 1983, Air Canada Flight 143 was to suffer a somewhat similar fate. At 132 tons, this three-month-old twin-engine Boeing 767 was a behemoth. To the casual observer, its cockpit glowed like it belonged in a video arcade. Loaded with screen upon screen of state-of-the-art computerized instruments, this was a plane that could seemingly fly itself. The most sophisticated jetliner of its time, it was the pride of the Canadian fleet.

Flight 143 departed from Montreal destined for Edmonton, with a brief stopover in Ottawa. The plane was certainly in very good hands. Captain Robert Owen Pearson was a twenty-six-year veteran with Air Canada. For years, Pearson had combined his career as a commercial pilot with work as a glider instructor and tow-plane operator. He and First Officer Maurice Quintal were among the few elite at the time who were trained to operate this incredible machine.

Along the final leg of the trip, the plane was flying at an altitude of 41,000 feet and everything seemed to be going just fine. Out of the blue, at 0109 Greenwich mean time, a warning light and one of those oh-so-annoying buzzer alarms suggested a problem with the forward pump in the left fuel tank. With two pumps in each of the plane's three fuel tanks, there was little cause for alarm. Redundancy was built into every aspect of the plane's operation. Then, suddenly, alarms went off indicating a problem with the second pump in the left-wing tank.

Uh, oh!

Without hesitation, Pearson contacted the Winnipeg Air Traffic Control Center with word of a problem. Flight 143 was immediately given clearance to land at Winnipeg, which was about 130 miles south of their location at that moment.

Things were only to get worse. Much worse.

Within five minutes of the first warning, alarms indicated that all six of the fuel pumps on the plane were failing. At nine minutes, the left engine failed. At twelve minutes, the right engine failed and the plane became powerless. The cockpit fell into total darkness and auxiliary power kicked in, only to die out shortly thereafter.

This was the worst possible scenario. Both engines had failed, the auxiliary power system had given out, and the plane was a long way from its destination. This was certainly one plane that was never designed to fly without power. While it wasn't falling out of the sky, it was pretty obvious that this plane was not going to stay up forever. The only thing that seemed to work in their favor was something called the ram air turbine, which used wind power to generate minimal hydraulic control. Clearly, Flight 143 had run out of fuel.

Calculations both within the cockpit and on the ground confirmed that without power, this plane was not going to make the Winnipeg airport. Instead, the decision was made to make an emergency landing at Gimli in Manitoba, an abandoned Royal Canadian Air Force base that had been equipped with twin 6,800-foot runways. Landing at Gimli did pose some additional risks, since the base lacked both a control tower and emergency equipment.

Would they make it? Could they make it? Even if they did, could the plane be controlled with enough precision to keep it from smashing into the ground or rolling over upon impact? No one knew the answers to these questions, but when you are faced with either making a very risky landing or death itself, the choice of what to do is very clear.

As the plane approached the Gimli airfield, the landing gear was released. Without any power to assist, the pilots were dependent on the force of gravity alone to lock the landing gear in place. The main landing gear fell into place without any problem. They weren't as lucky, however, with the nose gear. The onslaught of the wind beneath the plane prevented the front landing gear from locking into place. Now flying a powerless giant, the pilots were faced with the reality of landing it without all of the landing gear down.

If you thought that things couldn't get worse, just read on. . . .

The plane was coming in too high and risked overshooting the runway. In a move that was unheard of for a large aircraft, one that he had picked up from his gliding experiences, Pearson put the plane into a maneuver known as a sideslip. Although frightening to all aboard, it caused the plane to slow down and lose altitude, and Pearson brought the plane down within 200 feet of what would be considered a perfect landing.

The plane was down, but it had not stopped. Almost immediately, two tires in the right main landing gear popped and the casing of the right engine was scraping the pavement. Without the front nose gear in place, the belly of the plane was soon doing the same. Sparks were flying, but the increased force of friction actually helped to slow the plane down sooner.

There was also another unexpected problem. There were people in the middle of the runway! Unbeknownst to the pilots, the former runway was now the final straightaway of the two-kilometer Winnipeg Sports Car Club racecourse. Yes, you read it correctly. They had chosen to land on an active racetrack. People were scrambling for their lives.

All of a sudden, Pearson noticed a metal guardrail, which had been put in place for drag races, running right down the middle of the runway. He tried to veer the plane to the right side, but he had no luck. The left side of the plane's nose sheared the posts of the guardrail right off at their base. The plane finally came to a stop in a huge cloud of smoke. Amazingly, injuries from this near disaster were minimal and mostly caused during the evacuation of the plane.

So how did the plane run out of fuel?

Just like with my students, the error was basically in the math. Prior to the flight, the plane had experienced problems with its Fuel Quantity Indicating System, which basically controls the entire fueling process and all of its onboard fuel gauges. Generally, all the ground crew needs to do is to hook up the hoses and dial in how much fuel is needed. The computer does the rest. Since the plane was new, no spare parts were available to replace the faulty Fuel Quantity Processing Unit. The ground crew had to resort to calculating the fuel load by hand. They used the tried-and-true fuel-drip procedure, which is very similar to the dipstick that you have in your car to measure the amount of oil in the crankcase.

This manual accounting of the fuel led to another problem. The flight plan called for 22,300 kilograms of fuel, but the fuel trucks measured their fuel in liters. A multiplier of 1.77 was used to convert between the two units, but it was later learned that this was the wrong conversion factor. Instead of converting the liters to kilograms, they had calculated the number of imperial pounds. Since these were the first planes in the entire Air Canada fleet to use metric measurements, not a single person involved realized that the wrong multiplier was being used. Even though the drip test was repeated several times by different people, the conversion factor was so familiar that no one questioned its value. It was a number that they had all used over and over again in their calculations. This error, which was compounded by poor communication and training, allowed the plane to fly off with approximately half of the fuel that it actually needed to make its destination, and it almost proved deadly.

They say that history has a way of repeating itself, and this story is no exception. Eleven months to the day, on June 23, 1984, Captain Pearson and First Officer Quintal were once again behind the controls of the same exact plane on its way from Ottawa to Montreal. During takeoff, the same sequence of lights and buzzers indicated problems with the fuel pumps. When they leveled off, everything returned to normal. This time they were not taking any chances and immediately returned to the ground. It was later determined that they were in no danger. This time the plane had not run out of fuel. Instead, a false alarm had been generated by the plane's rapid ascent. (We can be sure that these guys were not happy campers. . . .)

The moral of this story? Watch those units! Failure to do so could have devastating consequences.

Useless? Useful? I will leave that for you to decide.

# sir alfred

## still there

My students always tell me that I seem to have a story for just about everything. So, when several of them told me that they were headed to France for spring break, I just couldn't let them down. I just had to tell them the strange story of a guy known as Sir Alfred, a man that had been stuck in a bureaucratic quagmire for more than a decade.

Now, Alfred wasn't his real name. His parents gave him the less noble title of Merhan Karimi Nasseri right after his birth in Iran in 1945. His father was an Iranian doctor and his mother a British nurse. In 1974, Nasseri left Iran to go to England. While he was there, his father died, and since his parents had never married, Nasseri's funding was cut off. Forced to return to Iran in 1977, Nasseri was arrested for participating in protests against the Shah and was expelled from Iran without a passport. He traveled around Europe for nearly four years, until he was granted refugee status in Belgium in 1981.

And he lived happily ever after. . . . Well, obviously not.

Nasseri decided to leave Belgium for Great Britain to search for relatives there. While on his way, he was mugged in a Paris train station. All of his papers proving that he was refugee living in Belgium were stolen.

Uh, oh!

When Nasseri arrived at Heathrow Airport in 1988, he was immediately sent back to France. Without a passport, the British authorities would not let him into the country. Upon his return to Paris, the French police tried to have him arrested for illegal entry, but without any papers, there was no evidence of what country to deport Nasseri to.

So there he sat, Nasseri taking up residence on one of those red plastic chairs in Terminal One of Charles de Gaulle Airport. In 1992, the French courts ruled that he had entered the airport legally as a political refugee and they could not toss him out of the country. Yet, the French denied Nasseri any type of visa, so he was not free to walk outside the terminal at any time.

Oddly, when the Belgian authorities first heard of his plight, they said Nasseri could have his documents reissued, but he had to come get them in person. Yet, without those documents in his hands, he was unable to travel to go get them. Talk about a catch-22 situation.

Then the Belgian government made a complete about-face. They outright refused to let him return under any circumstance. They argued that under Belgian law, those with refugee status that chose to leave the country automatically forfeited their rights.

In 1995, the Belgian authorities finally told Nasseri that he could return to Belgium and get his papers. The catch was that he had to live there under the supervision of a social worker. Nasseri refused and insisted that he would leave only if he could go to Great Britain.

It was this desire to go to England that got Nasseri his nickname. He had repeatedly applied for admittance to Great Britain but had no luck. Since the U.K.'s immigration forms had a space for an adopted name, Nasseri started writing in Alfred. He chose that pseudonym simply because he liked the name. The name stuck and people have been calling him Sir Alfred or just plain Alfred ever since.

Life may seem harsh being stuck in an airport for years, but Nasseri made good use of the little that was offered to him. He slept on an airport bench at night. During the day, he read books and magazines, wrote in his diary, and conversed with travelers. He was tidy and clean-cut, and washed in the men's room early in the morning before the passengers arrived. He refused to accept charity, although airport staff and stewardesses provided him with meal vouchers and complimentary travel kits. He never begged and would politely return lost wallets to their rightful owners.

Finally, in July 1999, the Belgian government agreed to send Sir Alfred his refugee papers. He was now free to leave. But eleven years of sitting in an airport can wreak havoc on a man's mind. It seems that Alfred no longer wanted to leave. The airport had become his home and he felt safe there. People treated him as a celebrity and he enjoyed the cards and letters that he received from all over the world.

And this is where my students entered the picture. Since they were traveling to France, I asked them to check to see if Sir Alfred was still there and to politely ask him if he would allow them to snap a picture of him. They asked around and confirmed that he was indeed still there, but he was in a different terminal. Upon their return, my students seemed disappointed that they were unable to meet the man whose plane seemed to be permanently delayed. Hopefully, by the time you read this, Sir Alfred will have reached his final destination.

Useless? Useful? I'll leave that for you to decide.

# the u.s. camel corps

## something seems just a little out of place here

It's hard to imagine the old West without images of the classic cowboy riding his horse off into the sunset. Yet, if things had gone differently, those old western movies would have had John Wayne riding into town on his camel. When the Lone Ranger was blurting out, "Hi-yo, Silver, away!" he would have been referring to his two-humped friend. And Roy Rogers would have had a dromedary named Trigger.

To see what I am talking about, we must set our timepieces back to the first part of the nineteenth century. At this time, the United States was undergoing a great expansion in size and most of the land that it obtained in the Southwest was desert. It was not a place for man, horses, or mules. Lack of water meant lack of life. Yet, the U.S. government was determined to explore this territory.

In 1836, Major George H. Crosman felt that he had the perfect solution. He proposed that the U.S. government purchase a bunch of camels. After all, what other animal was better suited for desert conditions? He was certain that this was the answer to their problem. Yet, like all good ideas, it fell on deaf ears. That was until Jefferson Davis, who was a Mississippi senator at the time, was told about the camel scheme. He regularly suggested the importation of camels to anyone that would listen, but, again, the idea went nowhere.

The tide began to change in 1853, when Davis was appointed secretary of war under President Franklin Pierce. Now he was in the position to recommend the purchase of camels. It took him another two years, but eventually Davis got the idea approved. On March 3, 1855, Congress appropriated $30,000 "to be expended under the direction of the War Department in the purchase and importation of camels and dromedaries to be employed for military purposes." The U.S. Army's Camel Corps was now officially in existence.

Now it was time to get some camels. There were none to be found in the United States, so Major Henry C. Wayne and Lieutenant David D. Porter were sent aboard the Navy ship *Supply* to the eastern Mediterranean to purchase some. Their knowledge of camels was minimal at best, so their first purchases were poor ones. Once they learned the ropes, they were able to obtain thirty-three of the animals at an average cost of $250 each. The camels were boarded on the ship for their three-month voyage across the sea.

From the moment the camels got on the ship, it was obvious that this plan was headed for failure. Knowing little about the care of camels, Wayne and Porter hired six Arabs and one Turk to make the journey to the United States. Just being born in the area, however, does not make you a camel expert. Like the Americans sent to get the camels, these guys basically knew nothing. The Turkish man, who was hired as the veterinarian, had one treatment for everything that ailed these animals: He tickled their noses with a chameleon tail. Clearly, he was well studied in veterinary medicine!

The ship finally arrived in Indianola, Texas, on May 14, 1856. One camel had died on the journey, but two were born along the way, so the team was ahead by one. Within minutes of unloading, however, there were problems. First, just the sight of the camels made the horses and mules go berserk. Second, they smelled really, really bad, and no one wanted to deal with them.

After some fattening up, the camels were placed at Camp Verde (near San Antonio, Texas) under the command of Lieutenant Edward F. Beale. We can be pretty certain that Beale, who had enlisted in the U.S. Navy at the age of fourteen, never dreamed he would be asked to lead a pack of dirty, smelly Army camels across the desert. Beale's mission was quite clear. He was to survey a route from Fort Defiance in New Mexico to eastern California along a trail that would someday become the western portion of that road where you could get your kicks—on Route 66. Clearly, this involved the crossing of a lot of desert terrain. This sounded like a job for . . . Underdog! No, wait a second. He would die of thirst also. No, this sounded like a job for the supercamels!

And off they went. At first, the camels struggled to keep up with the horse and mule teams. They may not have needed as much water, but, boy, were the camels slow! However, as in that classic race between the tortoise and the hare, you should always bet on the slow guy. After a few days, the camels adapted to their new environment and left the others in the dust.

When Beale completed his official report and submitted it to Congress, it was clear that the camel experiment was a great success. By this time, John B. Floyd had replaced Jefferson Davis as secretary of war and made the recommendation to Congress to import 1,000 more camels. It looked as if the western spotlight on the horse was about to fade into history.

Whoa! Not so fast! Hold your horses!

Making a recommendation is one thing. Actually getting the money to do it is another. You see, the United States had a big, big problem at the time. The country was on the verge of a civil war and the last thing Congress needed to deal with was a herd of camels.

Just in case you didn't know, there was a civil war. The two sides fought and fought and the United States eventually agreed to be purchased by AOL Time Warner. (Well, maybe not.) During the war, Camp Verde, which was still home to the camels that did not journey with Beale to California, fell under Confederate control and played absolutely no part in the war. The camels were treated very poorly, mainly because they were misunderstood. If there is one thing that a camel demands, it is R-E-S-P-E-C-T. Camels basically treat you the way you treat them. Hit them with a stick and they will spit on you. Kick them and they will kick you back. It was not unusual for a camel to "accidentally" get loose and have to fare for itself in the desert. As a result, the camels got the reputation of dirty, nasty, uncooperative animals. Few people had any use for these beasts.

When the war was over, Congress no longer had any interest in the camels. The railroad was expanding west, providing a much better means of transportation. The remaining camels were all auctioned off to the highest bidder, although interest was minimal. Many of these same camels were occasionally seen roaming the vast American desert as late as the beginning of the twentieth century. Unfortunately, the hatred against them was very high and many ranchers used the camels for target practice.

One of the Arabs originally hired for taking care of the camels, a man named Hadji Ali, whose name was Americanized as Hi Jolly, tried for many years to convince others how useful the animals could be. But even he had no success and was forced to let his camels go. Today, a monument stands in Arizona in tribute to Hi Jolly and the U.S. Camel Corps.

And so ended the grand camel experiment. It's hard to imagine how a plan that was so right could end up going so wrong.

Useless? Useful? I'll leave that for you to decide.

# the miracle man

## almost does count

Will Purvis is one of those people that history seems to have for-gotten. Will never accomplished anything more than the average man during his lifetime, yet luck was certainly on his side.

Our story begins with the birth of Will Purvis on September 27, 1872, in Jasper County, Mississippi. In 1884, the Purvis family picked up and moved to a farm about twelve miles northwest of Columbia, Mississippi. It was on this very farm at the age of nine-teen that the young Will Purvis would become infamous.

In 1893, Will joined a group called the White Caps, which was an order similar to the Ku Klux Klan. While attending his second White Caps meeting, Will learned from the group that a black servant named Sam Waller had recently switched jobs. Sam's previous employer was an elderly widow named Mrs. Hammond, but she was unable to pay him a competitive salary. Two brothers, Will and Jim Buckley, lured Sam away from Mrs. Hammond with the offer of a higher salary. In response to this apparent injustice, the White Caps took Sam and gave him a good whipping that they were sure he would never forget.

The flogging of Sam infuriated the Buckley brothers. They went to Columbia and brought the whole matter to the attention of the grand jury that was convening at the time. Three White Caps would eventually be indicted for the crime, but not before the White Caps met and cast a death lot against the Buckleys and their servant.

On June 22, 1893, upon their return from reporting the whipping, the three men were ambushed. Will Buckley was killed instantly and fell off his saddle to the ground. Jim Buckley watched the assassin jump into the woods and scramble. The assassin was identified by Buckley as Will Purvis.

Purvis was arrested that evening and was forced to walk the entire twelve miles to Columbia to appear before the grand jury. Purvis said that he was sitting at home on his porch after carrying wood into the kitchen when Buckley was murdered. He claimed that he'd quit the White Cap organization as soon as he'd learned that a white man was the target, and that he'd taken no part in the murder. He was quite confident that the accusation was just a mistake and that he would be released shortly thereafter.

Will Purvis could not have been more wrong. He was ordered to stand trial on the charges. Numerous witnesses were able to confirm that he was at home when the shooting took place, but that was countered with two pieces of compelling information. First, and most convincing, was the eyewitness testimony of Jim Buckley. This was followed by additional condemning evidence. Hounds had picked up the scent of the killer two days after the shooting. As cold as this trail may have seemed, experts claimed that it led directly to the Purvis farm.

Will Purvis was found guilty of first-degree murder and sentenced to die on September 6, 1893, between 11 A.M. and 3 P.M. The case went through the usual round of appeals up to the Mississippi Supreme Court, but the sentence was ultimately upheld.

On February 7, 1894, thousands of people gathered to watch the execution of Will Purvis. The Reverend Mr. Sibley read a passage of Scripture and then Purvis's hands were tied behind his back. When the sheriff asked him if he had anything to say, Will shouted, "I didn't do it." (There is some question as to the exact wording.) A black cap was placed over his head and the noose around his neck. The floor dropped and Will Purvis fell to his death.

Or maybe not.

Several minutes went by and Purvis regained consciousness. The exact reason for his survival is still debated today. Some claim that the executioner had cut off a frayed end of the rope and that it had become undone as Purvis fell. Others say that the rope simply snapped. There are even suggestions that the rope was greased.

Now that he had survived the hanging, the question came up as to what to do next. The crowd jeered to hang him again and Purvis was escorted back onto the platform. Before the second execution attempt was to take place, however, the Reverend Mr. Sibley climbed onto the scaffold and demanded that it be stopped. Claiming divine intervention, he asked anyone in the crowd that wished to see Purvis hanged again to raise his or her hand. No one did. Purvis was led back to jail to await a judicial decision on his case.

Once again, the case made it all the way up to the Mississippi Supreme Court, but in the end, it was decided that the principle of double jeopardy just didn't apply to a man already convicted of the crime. Purvis's punishment was execution and that was what should happen, no matter how many attempts it would take.

Although Purvis's second execution was scheduled for December 12, 1895, the execution was not to take place. On the eve of his hanging, friends helped Purvis escape from prison. He hid with friends and relatives under the worst of conditions. Living in constant fear of being caught, Purvis would later say that this was among the worst times of his life.

While on the lam, political conditions in Mississippi began to change. The case continued on in the public eye and became a hot issue in the upcoming gubernatorial race. The office went to A. J. McLaurin, who had campaigned on the promise of leniency in the case. As a result, Will Purvis turned himself in shortly after the inauguration and his sentence was reduced to life imprisonment.

Twenty-two months in hard labor went by before there was another weird twist in the case. Jim Buckley admitted publicly for the first time that he might have misidentified Will Purvis as his brother's murderer. This doubt, coupled with nearly 2,000 signatures requesting a pardon, left the governor with a tough decision to make. On December 19, 1898, Will Purvis was given a full pardon and released from prison the next day with a new suit of clothes and $10 in cash.

Will Purvis went on to become a prosperous farmer, a loving husband, and the father of eleven children. Most important of all, he was a law-abiding citizen for the rest of his life. Yet, there was always a dark cloud over Purvis's head. He knew that he was innocent but could not prove it to the rest of the world.

In 1917, a man named Joe Beard walked into a crowded revival meeting of the Holy Rollers. The pastor called on all sinners to come forward and cleanse their souls. Beard said little at the time but soon afterward became seriously ill. He admitted on his deathbed that he and a man named Louis Thornhill had murdered Will Buckley. Most important, he made it clear that Will Purvis had nothing to do with the murder. Purvis had told the truth; when the original idea of harming the Buckley brothers came to light, Purvis told his fellow White Caps that he wanted nothing to do with it and walked away.

In light of the new evidence clearing Purvis, on March 15, 1920, the Mississippi legislature awarded him $5,000 in compensation for "erroneous prosecution, conviction, and punishment." While Purvis was now a free man with a free conscience, Thornhill was never prosecuted for pulling the trigger that caused the death of Buckley. He got away on a legal technicality: Since Joe Beard died before a confession was signed and witnessed, it could not be entered as evidence in a court of law. Thornhill walked away without charges ever being pressed.

Will Purvis died on October 13, 1938. In another one of those strange twists of fate, Purvis died three days after the death of the last juror that had originally sentenced him to be executed.

Useless? Useful? I'll leave that for you to decide.

# the 1904 olympics

## these games were a sideshow in every sense

We usually have the image in our minds that the Olympics is really big business. The hosting cities go out of their way to make sure that everything runs smoothly and that the best facilities are provided for the competing athletes. But it wasn't always this way.

Take the 1904 St. Louis, Missouri, Summer Olympics, for example. These games were only the third summer games ever held. (There actually were no winter games at this time; they were added in 1924.) The original games were held in 1896 in Athens and were then followed by the 1900 Paris games.

The St. Louis games could hardly be called an international competition. Since traveling overseas from Europe was extremely expensive at the time, the competition consisted mostly of Americans and Canadians. In fact, of the 681 athletes, 525 were from the United States. Not a single athlete from England or France participated in the games. It should be pointed out, however, that the Olympics were not intended to be a competition among nations at the time. Instead, it was a competition among amateur athletes from around the world. It was the job of the amateur athletes to find their way to the games at their own expense. No one really cared if you couldn't get there.

Needless to say, the 1904 Olympics was of relatively minor importance to the world as a whole. They were originally scheduled to take place in Chicago, but President Teddy Roosevelt urged that the games be held in St. Louis because the Louisiana Purchase Exposition was being held there at the same time to showcase the world's newest technologies (electricity, automobiles, airplanes, etc.).

The exposition organizers built a permanent gymnasium and a stadium with enough seats to hold some 35,000 Olympic spectators. (This may sound like a lot of people, but it's really nothing when you compare it to the estimated 20 million people that attended the exposition during its six-month run.) The entire event lasted from Monday, August 29, to Saturday, September 3, 1904. There were no Olympic events scheduled for that Friday, so the entire series of games lasted for just five short days.

At this point, you probably don't see too much wrong with this scenario. Unfortunately, when the games were actually held, they were a disaster. The sideshows at a typical county fair are better organized.

To start, if you were considered to be a minority, you were expected to compete in separate games to show off your native skills. These events came under the high-sounding name of "Anthropology Days" and were held on August 12 and 13, 1904. These games were designed to pit "costumed members of the unciv-ilized tribes" against one another. Never-to-be-classic Olympic events were included: mud fighting, rock throwing, pole climbing, spear throwing, and . . . well, you get the idea.

Things went downhill from there.

In the swimming events, which were held in a lake, Hungary's Zoltan Halmay won the 100-meter and 50-meter freestyle. Originally, Halmay beat American J. Scott Leary by just one foot in the 50-meter event. However, the American judge ruled that Leary had won. This ruling resulted in a brawl between the two swimmers, so the judges ordered a rematch. Halmay won on the second attempt. (They couldn't check the videotape at this time in history.)

An American gymnast named George Eyser won one bronze, two silver, and two gold medals at the games. Quite a remarkable feat when you consider the fact that he only had one real leg—the other leg was solid wood. It seems that his leg had been amputated when he was run over by a train. Ouch!

Now for the competition that Olympic officials would really like to strike from the record books—the marathon.

The marathon was run on a very humid, ninety-plus-degree day. The forty-kilometer course started with five laps around the stadium track. The runners then left the stadium and embarked on a dusty, unpaved course that took them up and down over seven different hills. The path was marked by red flags that designated the way. A vanguard of horsemen cleared the trail along the way, followed by doctors, judges, and reporters in the newly invented automobiles. The net result was a constant cloud of dust kicked up into the runners' faces. They were literally forced to eat dust.

The first man to cross the finish line was Fred Lorz from New York City. Lorz had completed the race in just over three hours. When he entered the stadium, the crowd roared with excitement. Photographs were taken of President Roosevelt's daughter Alice placing a laurel wreath over Lorz's head.

Lorz's moment in the limelight did not last very long. Just as Lorz was about to accept his medal, officials learned that Lorz had been spotted passing the halfway mark in an automobile. It seems that Lorz had been suffering from cramps, so he hitched a ride at the nine-mile point. He waved at the spectators and fellow runners along the way. Lorz rode in the vehicle for eleven miles, at which point the car overheated and broke down. Lorz, now rejuvenated from his ride, chose to run the rest of the race.

Lorz claimed that he never meant to fool anyone; he just couldn't resist the praise and adulation of the roaring crowd. Lorz was immediately banned for life from any future amateur competition. (This ban was lifted a year later, allowing him to win the Boston Marathon. We'll assume that he was closely watched.)

So, if Lorz didn't win, who did?

It was a British-born man named Thomas Hicks, who ran for the American team. Hicks ran the race in 3:28:53. When he ran into the stadium, the crowd was less than enthusiastic. After all, they had already cheered for a winner, even if he had been disqualified.

Of course, good little Alice Roosevelt was again ready to pose with the winner. But she couldn't. Hicks had to be carried off the track. It seems that Hicks had begged to lie down about ten miles from the finish line. Instead, his trainers gave him an oral dose of strychnine sulfate mixed into raw egg white to keep him going. This was not enough; they had to give him several more doses, as well as brandy, along the way. By the end of the race, Hicks actually had to be supported by two of his trainers so he could cross the finish line. (Essentially, he was carried over the line with his feet moving back and forth.) Hicks was very close to death's door. It took four doctors to get him in good enough shape just to leave the grounds, after which he fell asleep on a trolley.

Wait! That's not the end of the story!

It seems that another entrant was a Cuban postman named Felix Carvajal. Once Carvajal heard about the marathon, he announced that he was going to run. He had no money, so he quit his job and went into the fund-raising business. He ran around the central square in Havana and jumped on a soapbox pleading for donations. He repeated this several times until he raised the cash necessary to come to the United States.

On his way to the race, Carvajal managed to lose all his money in a crap game in New Orleans. As a result, he had to hitchhike his way to the games, which was not an easy thing to do in 1904. When Carvajal arrived at the games, he lacked any type of running gear. The officials were forced to postpone the start of the marathon for several minutes while a New York City policeman cut the sleeves off Carvajal's shirt and the legs off Carvajal's pants. Carvajal ran the race in lightweight street shoes.

During the race, Carvajal didn't seem to fatigue easily. He constantly conversed with the crowd, even running backward at times while he spoke to the spectators in broken English.

But wait, in keeping with the 1904 tradition, it had to get worse for poor Felix Carvajal:

He blew any chance of victory by getting hunger pains. He first ate some peaches that he stole from a race official. He then took a detour into an orchard to munch on some green apples. Big mistake.

Carvajal developed stomach cramps and temporarily had to drop out of the marathon. He eventually got back in the race and managed to come in fourth place. He probably would have won if he had not gotten the munchies.

Hold it—the marathon is still not over!

The marathon included the first two black Africans to compete in the Olympics—two Zulu tribesmen named Lentauw (real name: Len Taunyane) and Yamasani (real name: Jan Mashiani). They wore bibs 35 and 36, respectively.

The only problem was that Lentauw and Yamasani were not in town to compete in the Olympics. They were actually the sideshow! Yes, they were imported by the exposition as part of the Boer War exhibit. (Both were really students from the Orange Free State province in South Africa, but no one wanted to believe that these men could actually be educated. It would have ruined the whole image.)

Lentauw finished ninth and Yamasani came in twelfth. This was a disappointment, as many observers were sure Lentauw could have done better. Unfortunately, he had been chased nearly a mile off course by a large, aggressive canine!

The marathon was over, but there is still one more little story to go along with this.

It seems that two of the patrolling officials driving in a brand-new automobile were forced to swerve to avoid hitting one of the runners. The officials ended up going down an embankment and were severely injured.

In the end, the St. Louis Olympics (along with the previous Paris games) proved to be such a disaster that the Olympic Committee, in an attempt to revive the flagging Olympic movement, was forced to hold interim Olympic Games in 1906 in Athens. These games were not numbered, but were attended by twenty countries and put the Olympics back on a steady course to success.

*An interesting useless sidenote:* Iced tea made its debut at the 1904 exposition. It seems that it was so hot during the expo that the staff at the Far East Tea House couldn't even give away their product.

What to do? What to do?

Very simple; they poured the hot tea over ice cubes! The drink quickly became the expo's most popular beverage.

*And yet another useless fact:* A teenager named Arnold Fornachou was selling ice cream at his exposition booth. He ran into a big problem; he ran out of paper bowls in which to serve the ice cream. In a stroke of genius, he noticed that the guy in the next booth, a Syrian named Ernest Hamwi, was selling waffles. Arnold rolled one of Ernie's wafer-thin waffles up and invented the ice cream cone. Within ten years, more than one-third of all ice cream was served in a cone.

Useless? Useful? I'll leave that for you to decide.

# it all comes with being human

# the bath school disaster

## the good old days weren't as good as you think

Let's do a time warp back to May 18, 1927, two days prior to the start of Lindbergh's historic crossing of the Atlantic. This particular day started out just like any other for the 700 or so residents of the village of Bath, Michigan. Yet, this day was not to be like any other. Around nine forty-five that morning, a tremendous explosion shook the community. Within just a short period of time, an additional loud blast would be heard.

At a time when radio was still in its infancy, news was very slow to spread, and area residents were unsure about what had just happened. The first explosion produced a giant cloud of smoke in one direction, yet there was a major fire burning in another. People followed their gut instinct and headed toward the source of the explosion. What they saw was something that we all hope never, ever, happens again. The community's five-year-old Bath Consolidated School, with more than 300 students enrolled, had just been blown to smithereens. With one-third of the school completely leveled, rescuers worked as fast as they could to pull the wounded and deceased out of the wreckage. Lifeless body after lifeless body was extracted. Panicked fathers joined in the search while mothers looked on with horror.

Just as things seemed as if they couldn't get any worse, a second explosion occurred about a half hour later. One of the cars near the disaster site blew up, killing the school's superintendent, a school board member, the village postmaster, and another man.

Rescuers, frantically searching through the portion of the school that was still standing, made a horrifying discovery and quickly called for everyone to get away from the building. The school was wired with over 500 pounds of dynamite, complete with a timer and a battery! Realizing the dynamite could go off at any moment, the rescuers carefully dismantled the explosives and removed them from the building.

We live in an age where we think that school shootings, bombings, and the like are only a modern phenomenon. It's not the type of thing that we would have expected to happen in the 1920s. How could such a thing have occurred? How could someone become so outraged that they would want to kill all of those innocent children?

The answer to these questions can be given with just one word: taxes.

It was all the doing of a man named Andrew P. Kehoe, who just happened to be one of the people killed in the automobile explosion outside the school. Kehoe was very upset that his taxes had dramatically increased in order to fund the construction of the new school. In an effort to reduce his tax levy, he ran for and was eventually elected to the community's board of education, where he quickly butted heads with the school's superintendent and other board members. His efforts to get his property taxes reduced were unsuccessful, however. Soon the higher taxes, coupled with increased medical expenses due to his wife's poor health, led to the foreclosure of Kehoe's farm.

Kehoe's frugal ways did not go unnoticed by the board. He convinced them to hire him to do some odd jobs around the school to avoid the cost of hiring an electrician. And what a wiring job he did. Not only did Kehoe perform his assigned duties, but he also spent weeks methodically wiring and setting up explosives around the school.

Witnesses said that a few minutes before the blast, they saw Kehoe leaving the school building and driving away. After an entire wing of the school was destroyed, Kehoe returned to the scene of the crime. Sitting in his pickup truck, he motioned Superintendent

Emory Huyck toward him. It is believed that the two men got into an argument and Kehoe pulled out a shotgun and blasted the rear seat of his truck, which was loaded with his remaining explosives. Kehoe, Huyck, and three others were killed instantly.

The next morning, the body of Kehoe's wife was found at their farm. Her husband had apparently killed her prior to the bombing of the school. He had wired his home and outbuildings with explosives timed to go off after he left for the school. All of the buildings on his farm were burned to the ground.

In the end, Kehoe had killed a total of forty-five people. This included two teachers, the superintendent, the postmaster, a retired farmer, Kehoe, his wife, and thirty-eight children, most between the ages of six and eight. More than fifty others were injured.

As hard as it is to imagine, the death toll from the blast could have been much worse. It was later determined that a short circuit prevented the rest of the school from exploding. Also, the blast occurred during final exams at the school, so the older students were not scheduled to arrive until later that morning.

After all of the victims were laid to rest, the villagers were faced with the task of rebuilding their school. Since they were still paying for the school that was destroyed, the increase in taxes to cover the new construction would have put many of its residents into bankruptcy. Luckily, the state came to the rescue with disaster relief, and the school was rebuilt. Today, the replacement school has been torn down and a park commemorates those that lost their lives to the actions of one deranged man.

This awful tragedy still ranks as the most deadly act of school violence in American history. Much of the world has long forgotten this story, but it is a tragic event that will never be forgotten by the residents of Bath.

Useless? Useful? I'll leave that for you to decide.

# Ota Benga

## the guy that lived in a cage at the zoo

How many times have you heard people complain about how bad their life is? They are down in the dumps because their beaus left, they lost their jobs, or, even worse, their mommies wouldn't buy them candy. Well, the next time you hear someone say how bad things are, you should tell them the story of Ota Benga. His life was bad. Really bad. And no matter how bad your life may seem, it will never be as bad as Ota's was.

Ota's story goes back to 1903, when the folks setting up the 1904 Louisiana Purchase Exposition/Olympics decided that they wanted to display some African Pygmies in their native habitat as a part of the anthropology exhibit. As you probably know, Africa is a long way across the giant sea from St. Louis.

This is where a guy named Samuel Verner enters the picture. Verner was one of those part missionary, part explorer, part anthropologist, and part "out to earn some bucks" type of guys. On his previous trip to Africa, he'd returned with two African men named Kassongo and Kondola, whom he'd enrolled in the Stillman Institute in Tuscaloosa, Alabama. (Kassongo was later killed in the Shiloh Church disaster.)

In the eyes of bigwigs at the exposition, Verner seemed like the perfect candidate to get the job done. He was given a cash advance, an official title, and a shopping list of sorts. Yet, this particular shopping list was not typical at all. He wasn't headed to the market for some milk and eggs. Instead, Verner was contracted to bring back twelve Pygmies (all to meet particular sex, age, and status specifications) and an additional six Africans from other tribes, as well as all of the supplementary materials needed to reproduce their living environment in the United States. Verner and Kondola set sail and, after a brief stopover in Europe for supplies, arrived in Africa in mid-January 1904.

This was not a good time for one to make a visit to Africa. The Europeans were in a fierce, one-sided battle with the people of the Congo to colonize the land in order to gain access to its vast resources, particularly rubber. It has been estimated that as many as 10 million Africans lost their lives during this European conquest.

Which leads us to Ota Benga. Ota just happened to be out hunting for several days when his village was invaded. Upon his return home, Ota discovered that the Belgian-paid Force Publique had butchered his entire hunting band, his wife, and his children. By the time Verner entered the village of the Baschilele people in March, the destitute Ota had become a part of the African slave trade and was on the market to be sold. Verner was able to buy Ota's freedom for just a pound of salt and a few yards of cloth. With no family or hunting clan to return to, Ota volunteered to accompany Verner back to the United States. Verner was able to persuade just four other Pygmies to go to America, far short of the number his contract called for.

You are probably thinking that things could not get much worse for poor Ota Benga. There surely could be nothing more horrific than losing your family and everything that is important to you. But life was only going to get worse for Ota. And if worse wasn't bad enough, it would eventually become downright awful.

Read on. . . .

Upon their arrival at the St. Louis Exposition, Ota and the other Pygmies essentially became part of a carnival sideshow. Although described as an exercise in anthropology, the exhibition was nothing more than pure exploitation. The Pygmies were encouraged to snap their sharpened teeth at onlookers, to perform their native dances, and to compete in the "Anthropology Days" portion of the Olympics. When the autumn air set in, they were refused proper clothing because the anthropologists felt it would interfere with their body's normal cooling functions. (It never occurred to these scientists that the Pygmies came from a much warmer region and had no need for clothing back home. Duh!) The newspapers did not help the situation by stating that the Pygmies were cannibals, enjoyed torturing animals, and lacked intelligence.

At the end of the exposition, the Pygmies were asked if they wanted to stay in the United States. You can probably figure out that this was not a tough decision for the Pygmies to make. After considering all of the wonderful things that the United States had offered them, they couldn't think of any reason to stay, so within a few seconds, they all asked to be returned to their homeland. The exposition organizers agreed and arranged for Verner to take them back to Africa.

Upon their return, each went his or her separate way. Verner went about trying to strike it rich, while the Pygmies tried to adapt back to everyday life. (Just think of the stories that the Pygmies must have told about America. . . .) Ota remarried and it looked as if his life was finally going to be great. Soon, however, tragedy struck again. Ota's second wife was bitten by a poisonous snake and died. Ota was a widower for the second time. With nothing left to live for, Ota asked Verner to take him back to the United States so he could start a new life there. Verner agreed and the two arrived in New York City in August 1906.

But things didn't go as originally planned. Verner had amassed a large collection of artifacts and animals to sell in the United States. Verner's asking prices, however, were too high, and the museums balked. Eventually, the creditors came calling. Verner had no choice but to leave Ota in the care of the American Museum of Natural History while he went south trying to earn some much-needed cash.

Ota was actually left in very good hands at the museum. He was given street clothes and allowed to wander the museum freely. Ota blended right in, but in time he became restless. For a guy raised on the beauty and freedom that nature afforded, the confines of the museum were sorely lacking. Ota was that proverbial fish out of water. The museum's director requested that Verner arrange for an alternative place for Ota to stay.

Ota's next stop was the place that would gain him a place in history. On the voyage over from Africa, Ota had cared for a chimpanzee named Dohong, which Verner later sold to the Bronx Zoo for $275. Unable to care for Ota, Verner asked the zoo's director, William Temple Hornaday, if Ota could stay on and help out as best he could. For the first couple of weeks, Ota wandered the zoo in street clothes and hardly anyone took notice of him. But a trap was being set. The keepers allowed Ota access to Dohong's cage whenever he desired. He was then encouraged to set up his hammock in the cage. Next, Ota was given a bow and some arrows and encouraged to shoot at a target set up within the metal bars. Somehow, Ota had gone from helping with an exhibit to actually becoming the exhibit itself. Bones were scattered around the cage to add a sense of cannibalism. A sign was posted on the enclosure that read:

THE AFRICAN PYGMY, "OTA BENGA."

AGE, 28 YEARS. HEIGHT, 4 FEET 11 INCHES.

WEIGHT 103 POUNDS. BROUGHT FROM THE KASAI RIVER,

CONGO FREE STATE, SOUTH CENTRAL AFRICA,

BY DR. SAMUEL P. VERNER.

EXHIBITED EACH AFTERNOON IN SEPTEMBER.

You are probably feeling a sense of outrage right now. Yet, few people felt that way back then. On September 9, 1906, the *New York Times* printed the first story about the man living in the Monkey House. The headline simply read, "Bushman Shares a Cage with Bronx Park Apes." The public was hooked and the crowds started gathering. Attendance shot through the roof and Hornaday knew that he had stumbled on a cash cow.

Eventually, controversy started to brew in two different arenas. Once the leaders of the black community became aware of the situation, there was an immediate uproar. A lot of noise was made, but few listened. The real debate over Ota began with those citizens that were fundamentally opposed to Darwin's theory of evolution. By placing in a cage a Pygmy who was small in stature and considered to be lacking intelligence, there was the implied sense that Ota was the missing link between man and ape. This just could not continue.

All this building pressure actually did little to sway Hornaday. Although the sign was removed, Ota remained the main attraction at the zoo. It was actually Ota himself that quickly brought an end to this ridiculous situation. He couldn't stand the constant prodding, teasing, and staring of the crowds and started to create some mischief that found its way right into Hornaday's office. One day, the whole thing came to a head. Ota's keepers had discovered him playing with some children and began to spray the poor guy with a hose. Ota responded by ripping off his clothes. The keepers, of course, tried to force Ota to put his clothes back on. Ota ran off and returned swinging a knife and was finally locked back in the cage. On September 25, the *New York Times* ran another story, titled "Benga Tries to Kill; Pygmy Slashes at Keeper Who Objected to His Garb." This news threw the eggs right into Hornaday's face and brought a swift end to Ota's time as a zoo specimen.

On September 27, Ota left the Bronx Zoo for good. He was placed in the hands of the Howard Colored Orphan Asylum. The facility was run by the Reverend James H. Gordon, perhaps the man who protested the loudest about the zoo situation. He worked to teach Ota to read, write, and speak English but met with only limited success. What actually happened while Ota was there remains in question (it has been reported that he had intimate relations with a younger woman), but in January 1910, the orphanage severed ties with Ota.

Ota found his way to the Baptist Seminary in Lynchburg, Virginia, and seemed to adapt well to his new life. His name was Americanized to Otto Bingo, he dressed in American type clothing, and he even had his pointed teeth capped. He became a Christian and requested a baptism. Ota worked some odd jobs like sorting tobacco, feeding chickens, and maintaining grounds, but he still had a strong passion for the wilderness and hunting.

On March 20, 1916, Ota lit a fire and stripped down to his loin-cloth. He broke the caps off his teeth. Like many times before, a crowd of boys gathered to watch him singing and dancing around the fire. This time, however, Ota chased them away. He then pulled out a gun and shot himself through the heart. Ota was now at peace.

This may not be the last that you will ever hear about the sad life of Ota Benga. Hollywood has announced the production of a major motion picture with Denzel Washington as its producer. Whether the movie is ever made and what role Denzel will play in the making of the movie is something that only time will tell. One thing that we can be sure of is that Denzel will not have the lead role. He's just a tad bit too tall. The only way he could pull that off would be to do one of Tim Conway's "Dorf" tricks, which just wouldn't play well on the silver screen.

Useless? Useful? I'll leave that for you to decide.

# murderous mary

## the day mary, the elephant, was hanged

The story that I am about to tell you is one that certainly happened, but the exact details are lost to history. As the title suggests, this is the story of Mary, the elephant, and the day that she was hanged. There is no question as to whom Mary murdered, where it was done, or how Mary was finally executed; all witnesses generally agree upon those details. The minor points, on the other hand, are lost in years of countless retellings and rewritings of the legend.

Our story begins on September 11, 1916, in St. Paul, Virginia. Here we find a man named Walter "Red" Eldridge working as a janitor at the Riverside Hotel. Red, who was described by many to be a drifter, felt that he had nothing to lose by signing up with the circus that was visiting the town. There was no way that Red could have known that this was to be a fateful decision. Yes, this was to be Red's last full day here on earth.

The circus that captured Red's heart was the soon-to-be infamous Sparks World Famous Shows, which was owned by, of course, the one and only Charlie Sparks. While not the smallest circus of its day, it was far from the largest or most prestigious in the world. At a time when the quality of a circus show was determined solely by the number of rolling railroad cars and elephants, Charlie could not compete with the big guys. Charlie's circus had just ten railroad cars and five elephants to its name, which was far fewer than his nearest competitor.

Charlie, however, did have one feather in his cap. A rather large feather, in fact. Her name was Mary, and she was considered to be the largest elephant in captivity at the time. Billed as being three inches taller than Barnum's world-famous Jumbo, Mary weighed in at just a little over five tons. Just like Red's past, little was known about Mary's history. Some claimed that Charlie purchased her while she was still a baby. Others claimed that she had killed several people and after each killing, her name was changed and she was sold off to another circus.

Red's first day with the circus went fairly well. He was placed in charge of caring for a smaller elephant, and the circus performed two shows that day. Everything was then packed up and shipped down to the next stop, Kingsport, Tennessee. Kingsport, a relatively new town, was undergoing immense economic growth at the time and was certainly a great place to earn some cash.

The first show in Kingsport went off without a hitch. Prior to the next show, the elephants were marched about a half mile to the nearest watering hole. Red was placed in charge of Mary and what happened next is not clearly known.

In the most popular version of the story, Mary reached for a watermelon rind with her trunk. Red prodded Mary with his elephant stick, but Mary continued to try to get the delectable treat. Red then whacked Mary with the stick and she reacted quite instinctively. She grabbed Red with her trunk and threw him to the ground.

*(Warning!!! For those with weak stomachs, you may wish to skip the next sentence.)*

Mary then walked over to Red and, with one step, crushed his skull.

*(End of warning!!! You can continue reading. . . .)*

The onlookers all scrambled to avoid being Mary's next victim.

Sadly, as you have probably already concluded, poor Red Eldridge was to be no more.

People started chanting to kill Mary, but Charlie Sparks was not about to destroy an elephant supposedly worth in excess of $8,000. In fact, her popularity was confirmed later that evening when Mary performed in the second Kingsport show. Attendance skyrocketed! It seemed like everyone wanted to see the killer elephant.

But Sparks had a big dilemma on his hands. Word spread quickly about Mary's murderous rampage, and the next towns that the circus was scheduled to visit made it very clear that Mary was not welcome. The cry for Mary's head continued to grow louder.

What to do? What to do?

Charlie Sparks came to the inevitable conclusion that Mary had to be destroyed. Keeping her alive would kill his business. But if he was going to kill her, it had to be done in typical circus fashion. Her demise needed to be a spectacle.

Different ideas were tossed around. Mary could be electrocuted, but no neighboring town had enough juice to do it. A bullet might do the trick, but it was generally agreed that no bullet could penetrate her thick skin.

The final decision was to hang Mary. Clearly, the typical hangman's noose was not going to work here. Mary was to be carted off to the town of Erwin for the dirty deed to be done. There, the Clinchfield Railroad had its 100-ton derrick car in the train yard. Designed for lifting wrecked railroad cars and locomotives, this machine would certainly have no problem with Mary.

Or would it?

At 4 P.M. on Wednesday, September 16, 1916, a big crowd, with estimates ranging from 3,000 to 5,000 people (at least we can be sure that it was more than one), gathered at the Clinchfield rail yard to witness the hanging of Mary, the elephant.

*(Warning! You'd better turn away again!)*

The first step was to chain Mary's leg to the rail to keep her from harming anyone while they placed the crane in position. A chain was lowered from the derrick's boom and wrapped around Mary's neck.

Slowly, the crane started to pull and the chain tightened. Mary's front legs lifted five or six feet off the ground and then . . .

Snap!

Someone had forgotten to release Mary's leg that was still chained to the ground, and the tension caused the chain around

Mary's neck to break violently. Mary crashed to the ground. Crowd members once again scrambled for their lives, but it was soon realized that Mary wasn't going anywhere. She had broken her hip in the fall.

A heavier chain was then placed around her neck and, after taking her last breath, Mary was left hanging for all to see. Her body was eventually lowered into a pit near the rail yard, although its exact location was never marked and remains unknown.

*(Okay, the gruesome details have all passed. We now rejoin our story, already in progress.)*

Today, an event like this could never happen. It's just downright cruel and even painful to imagine. Yet, we can't change history. We can be pretty sure that there are people in Erwin, Tennessee, that wish it had never happened. To this day, the town is best known for its execution of Mary, the elephant.

Useless? Useful? I'll leave that for you to decide.

# charles ponzi

## double your money in ninety days

Have I got a deal for you! I can double your money in just ninety days, guaranteed.

"Nonsense!" you say.

What? You don't trust me? I promise you that it can be done. A man named Charles Ponzi delivered on such a promise back in 1920.

Now, I know what you are thinking. This has to be some type of scam. Well, I would be lying if I said that it wasn't. (Put your money back in the bank. You're not getting rich this week.)

**How It All Started**

Carlo "Charles" Ponzi was born in Parma, Italy, in 1882 and then immigrated to the United States in November 1903. Over the next fourteen years, Ponzi wandered from city to city and from job to job. He worked as a dishwasher, waiter, store clerk, and even as an Italian interpreter. In 1917, he settled back in Boston where he took a job typing and answering foreign mail. It was here in Boston on that fateful day in August 1919 that Ponzi discovered the mechanism to make both him and his investors very wealthy.

At the time, Ponzi was considering issuing an export magazine. He had written a letter about the proposed publication to a gentleman in Spain, and when Ponzi received the gentleman's reply, the man had included an international postal coupon. The idea behind this enclosure was quite simple: Ponzi was to take the coupon to his local post office and exchange it for American postage stamps. He would then use those American stamps to send a copy of the magazine to Spain when published.

Ponzi noticed that the postal coupon had been purchased in Spain for about one cent in American funds. Yet, when he cashed it in, he was able to get six American one-cent stamps. Just think of the possibilities if you could do this. You could buy $100 worth of stamps in Spain and then cash them in for $600 worth of stamps in the United States. Then cash in or sell the stamps to a third party, and you have, well, good old cash. You just couldn't get this kind of interest in the bank.

Ponzi's mind quickly went into overdrive, and he devised a clever scheme to capitalize on his idea. He was determined to be a rich man. His first step was to convert his American money into Italian lire (or any other currency where the exchange rate was favorable). Ponzi's foreign agents then used these funds to purchase international postal coupons in countries with weak economies. The stamp coupons were then exchanged back into a favorable foreign currency and finally back into American funds. Ponzi claimed that his net profit on all these transactions was in excess of 400 percent.

Was he really able to do this? The answer is a definite no. The red tape involved in dealing with the various postal organizations, coupled with the long delays in transferring currency, ate away at all Ponzi's imagined profits.

## Things Got Just a Bit out of Hand

A failed scheme couldn't keep Ponzi from bragging about his great idea. Friends and family members easily understood what he was saying and they wanted in on the investment. And, let's face it, if you flash money in people's faces, they are bound to take it.

On December 26, 1919, Ponzi filed an application with the city clerk establishing his business as the Security Exchange Company. He promised 50 percent interest in ninety days, and the world wanted in on it. Yet, he claimed to be able to deliver on his promise in just forty-five days. This, of course, translated into being able to double investors' money in just ninety days. Word spread very quickly about Ponzi's great idea, and within a few short months, the lines outside the door of his School Street office began to grow. Thousands of people purchased Ponzi promissory notes at values ranging from $10 to $50,000. The average investment was estimated to be about $300. (That was a big chunk of pocket change in those days.)

You are probably sitting there puzzled. Why would so many people invest in a scheme that didn't work? The reason was that the early investors did see great returns on their money. Ponzi used the money from later investors to pay off his earlier obligations. It was a new twist on the age-old pyramid scheme. With an estimated income of $1 million per week at the height of his scheme, his newly hired staff couldn't take the money in fast enough. They were literally filling all of the desk drawers, wastepaper baskets, and closets in the office with investors' cash. Branch offices opened and copycat schemes popped up across New England.

By the summer of 1920, Ponzi had taken in millions and started living the life of a very rich man. He purchased a twenty-room Lexington mansion, dressed in the finest suits, had dozens of gold-handled canes, and showered his wife in fine jewels.

## The Crash

Any get-rich scheme is certain to attract the attention of the law, and Ponzi's was no exception. From the start, federal, state, and local authorities investigated him, yet no one could pin Ponzi with a single charge of wrongdoing. Ponzi had managed to pay off all of his notes in the promised forty-five days, and since the investors were happy to get their earnings, not a single complaint had been filed. On July 26, 1920, however, Ponzi's house of cards began to collapse. The *Boston Post* headlined a story on the front page questioning the legitimacy of Ponzi's scheme. Later that day, the district attorney somehow convinced Ponzi to suspend taking in new investments until an auditor examined the books. (Why anyone who was doing something so highly illegal would let auditors examine his books is beyond me.)

Within hours, crowds of people were lined up outside Ponzi's door demanding their investments back. Ponzi obliged and assured the public that his organization was financially stable, and that he could meet all obligations. He returned the money to those who requested it. By the end of the first day, he had settled nearly 1,000 claims with the panicked crowd. By continuing to meet all of his obligations, the angry masses began to dwindle and public support swelled. Crowds followed Ponzi's every move. He was urged by many to enter politics and was hailed as a hero. Loud cheers and applause were coupled with people eager to touch his hand and assure him of their confidence.

And Ponzi continued to dream. He planned to establish a new type of bank where the profits would be split equally between the shareholders and the depositors. He also planned to reopen his company under a new name, the Charles Ponzi Company, whose main purpose would be to invest in major industries around the world. (Apparently, no one ever told Ponzi that the key to any successful swindle was to take the money and run.)

The public continued to support him until August 10, 1920. On this date, the auditors, banks, and newspapers declared that Ponzi was definitely bankrupt. Two days later, Ponzi confessed that he had a criminal record, which worsened his situation. It was revealed that in 1908 he had served twenty months in a Canadian prison on forgery charges related to a similar high-interest scheme. This was followed in 1910 by an additional two-year sentence in Atlanta, Georgia, for smuggling five Italians over the Canadian border into the United States.

On August 13, Ponzi was finally arrested by federal authorities and released on $25,000 bond. Just moments later, he was rearrested by Massachusetts authorities and rereleased on an additional $25,000 bond.

In the End . . .

The whole thing turned into one gigantic mess. There were federal and state civil and criminal trials, bankruptcy hearings, suits against Ponzi, suits filed by Ponzi, and the ultimate closing of five different banks.

Of course, we cannot forget the problem of trying to settle Ponzi's accounts in an attempt to return all of the people's investments. An estimated 40,000 people had entrusted an estimated $15 million (about $140 million in U.S. funds today) in Ponzi's scheme. A final audit of his books concluded that he had taken in enough funds to buy approximately 180 million postal coupons, of which they could only actually confirm the purchase of two. Ponzi's only legitimate source of income was $45 that he received as a dividend of five shares of telephone stock. His total assets came to $1,593,834.12, which didn't come close to paying off the outstanding debt. It took about eight years, but note holders were eventually able to have an estimated 37 percent of their investment returned in installments. In other words, many people lost big time.

Ultimately, Ponzi was sentenced to five years in federal prison for using the mails to defraud. After three and a half years in prison, Ponzi was sentenced to an additional seven to nine years by Massachusetts's authorities. He was released on $14,000 bond pending an appeal and disappeared about one month later.

Poof! Ponzi was gone. Where did he go? Did he leave the country? Did he just vanish off of the face of the earth? Was he bumped off by an angry client? No one was really sure.

Ponzi turned up a short time later in Florida. Under the assumed name of Charles Borelli, Ponzi was involved in a pyramid (big surprise, huh?) land scheme. He was purchasing land at $16 an acre, subdividing it into twenty-three lots, and selling each lot off at $10 a piece. He promised all investors that their initial $10 investment would translate into $5,300,000 in just two years. Forget doubling your money in ninety days; Ponzi was now promising even greater returns! Too bad much of the land was underwater and absolutely worthless.

Ponzi was indicted for fraud and sentenced to one year in a Florida prison. Once again, he jumped bail, on June 3, 1926, and ran off to Texas. He hopped a freighter headed for Italy but was captured on June 28 in a New Orleans port. On June 30, he sent a telegram to President Calvin Coolidge asking to be deported. Ponzi's request was denied, and he was sent back to Boston to complete his jail term. Ponzi was released early for good behavior after seven years and deported to Italy on October 7, 1934. Believe it or not, even after all of his swindling, he still had many fans who were there to give him a rousing send-off.

Back in Rome, Ponzi became an English translator. Mussolini then offered him a position with Italy's new airline, and he served as the Rio de Janeiro branch manager from 1939–1942. Then Ponzi discovered that several airline officials were using the carrier to smuggle currency. He wanted a cut of the action. When they refused to include him, he tipped off the Brazilian government. The Second World War brought about the airline's failure, and Ponzi soon found himself unemployed. Once again, he wandered from job to job. He tried running a Rio lodge, but that failed. He then alternated between earning a pittance providing English lessons and drawing from the Brazilian unemployment fund.

Ponzi died in January 1949 in the charity ward of a Rio de Janeiro hospital. Somehow, the man who had gone from pauper to multimillionaire and right back to pauper in a matter of six months had managed to save up $75 to cover the costs of his burial. He left behind an unfinished manuscript appropriately titled "The Fall of Mister Ponzi" and is immortalized by the expression "Ponzi scheme." And what a rise and fall it was.

Useless? Useful? I'll leave that for you to decide.

# the new english

## good luck understanding this one

While recently walking through my local supersized, humongous, can't-find-anything bookstore, I stopped to take a good look around. Aisle after aisle, shelf upon shelf, the books were piled sky high. All these books were the result of endless hours of hard work by aspiring authors. It quickly occurred to me how little chance there was of ever writing a real classic. Millions of different books have been cranked out, but only a handful can be remembered after even a few years.

In my mind, there are basically two ways to create a classic. You could create something so fantastic, so original, and so creative that no one will ever stop talking about it. Or, you could take the complete opposite approach. You could create a work that is so bad, so really bad, so really, really *bad,* that no one will ever stop talking about it. Either way, you get the same exact effect in the end.

Since most of us are not literary geniuses, clearly the second method is the best way to go. Take the work of Portuguese author Pedro Carolino as a good example of this latter method of writing a classic.

Carolino was one of those authors who set out with the best of intentions to create a great book. We can be sure that he did his homework, spent endless hours finalizing the manuscript, and felt great excitement to actually see his finished work published.

Yes, Carolino's work went on to become a classic, but for all the wrong reasons. His book, originally titled *The New Guide of the*

*Conversation in Portuguese and English,* was intended to be the definitive Portuguese-English phrase book. You know this type of book well. You need to go to the bathroom in some foreign land, so you pull out your phrase book for assistance. A little fumbling through the pages and you find, "Where is the bathroom?" Then, with the added effect of your bad accent, you tell the guy, "Where is the foot in your mouth located?" He then slugs you.

People using Carolino's phrase book suffered a similar fate. It seems that Carolino had little command of the English language, so he was off to a bad start. Even worse, he lacked a Portuguese-English dictionary.

In most people's eyes, this would be an insurmountable obstacle. You want to write the ultimate Portuguese-English phrase book, but you don't speak the language or have a basic dictionary to provide translations.

But this did not stop Carolino. No way, indeed. Instead, Carolino took an alternate approach. He was able to get his hands on both a Portuguese-French and a French-English dictionary.

You can see where this is going. . . .

Carolino took his Portuguese expressions and first translated them into French using the first dictionary. Then, he translated the phrases from French to English using the second reference.

So, how did it turn out? Let's just say that if it had turned out well, the book would have long been forgotten to history. Just to give you an idea of how disastrous this project turned out, let's look at some of the phrases that are supposedly common to the English language:

- *Let us go respire the air.*
- *At what o'clock is to get up?*
- *Apply you at the study during that you are young.*
- *Bring in dinner the beef.* (Perhaps the precursor to "Where's the beef?")
- *These apricots and these peaches make me and to come water in mouth.*
- *Give me some good milk newly get out.*

- *He do the devil at four.* (And will burn for eternity for this dastardly deed.)
- *He was wanting to be killed.*
- *He caresses all women.* (Can one go to jail for this?)
- *I please me self in the country.* (Use your imagination here. . . .)
- *I dead myself in envy to see her.*
- *I take a broth all morning.* (Must be a big pot.)
- *The lodestone attract to himself the iron.*
- *One she is ugly; at least she is gracious.* (A compliment?)
- *Keep the chestnut of the fire with the cat foot.* (???)

Carolino did not just limit his book to popular phrases. He also included pages of typical conversations in English. Take this dialogue between the traveler and a banker as an example:

[Traveler]: I have the honour to present you a ex-change letter, draw on you and endorsed to my order.

[Banker]: I can't accept it seeing that I have not nor the advice neither funds of the drawer.

[Traveler]: It has not yet happened it is at usance.

[Banker]: I know again the signature and the flourish of my correspondent; I will accept him to the day of the falling comprehend there the days of grace, if at there to that occasion I shall received theirs orders.

[Traveler]: In this case, I not want of to do to protest it.

[Banker]: It can to spare him the expenses of the protest.

[Traveler]: Will you to discharge this other trade what there is it? It is payable to the sight.

[Banker]: Yes, I will pat it immedeatly, I go to count you the sum.

[Traveler]: Would you have so good as to give me some England money by they louis?

[Banker]: With too much pleasure.

Clearly, the two people involved in this conversation have no problem understanding each other. Unfortunately, however, no one who actually speaks English has any clue what is going on. (Actually, many of the translated conversations in the book can be followed to some degree.)

My favorite section is one called "Idiotisms and Proverbs." You and I both probably know that he meant *idioms,* but if you use any of these expressions in an English-speaking country, *idiotisms* is probably a more appropriate word.

The original 1883 publication of this book in the United States featured an excellent introduction by Mark Twain. He was able to sum up the book with just one sentence: "One cannot open this book anywhere and not find richness."

You can't help but wonder if Carolino ever fully understood how inaccurate his book was. It is clear that he never set out to create such a masterpiece. Only the complete screwups can attain that level of fame. We can be pretty sure that he did earn some money from it. The U.S. edition was actually a reprint of the *second* edition of the book. It was quite popular at the end of the nineteenth century and continues to be republished every thirty years or so.

Useless. Useful? I'll leave that for you to decide.

PART 5

# hmmm . . .

# murphy's law

## it figures

I don't know why it is, but I always seem to check out my purchases at the store at the worst moment. First, the store is packed. Of course, only one line is open and someone very slow is running the register.

It has become clear to me that these stores operate under a principle that is secretly known as the Six-Million-Dollar-Man-Swipe (SMDMS). For the SMDMS to be properly executed, the cashier must swipe the product past the scanner in incredibly slow motion to simulate high speed. (If you have never seen the TV show, you probably have no clue what I am talking about.) The net effect is that you are supposed to get out of the supermarket sooner. According to the SMDMS training manual, if the cashier moves the product at an imperceptible speed past the laser beam, time will actually start to move backward. Yes, you will actually leave the line before you get on it. And, I bet that you see this all of the time. People walk up to the checkout and notice the incredibly long line. All of a sudden, they are gone. So, the supermarket's conclusion is that the SMDMS has worked and there is no need to hire additional staff. One very slow checkout is all that they need.

Of course, not all retail stores are well versed in the SMDMS. Some operate on the technique that I always seem to stumble upon. It just happened to me the other day at the local CVS while I was trying to buy a simple pack of cough drops.

Zip. In and out.

Well, I figured wrong. I fell into the latest of checkout schemes. To save money, the CVS operated only one checkout line. Of course, stupid me decided to get on the line with my pack of cough drops. The line just kept getting longer and longer while the manager stood there on the side with her arms crossed. Apparently, having the highest-paid worker in the store standing around doing absolutely nothing helps make the store more profitable. And here is where I stumbled onto the latest in checkout technology, called YEUL, which is an acronym for You End Up Last. Here's how YEUL works if it is carried out according to the rule book: First, you must end up smack-dab in the middle of a very long line when the arms-crossed manager finally decides that it is time to open another register. The person that is last in line runs and becomes the first in the newly formed line. The person that was second to last in the original line is now second in the new line, and so on. And, to make this plan work to its fullest, the person in the middle of the original line (almost certainly me!) ends up in the back. The mad rush for the checkout dies down, no one else gets on line behind me, and I end up being the very last person to check out.

Curiosity finally got the best of me a couple of years ago, and I decided that it was time to find out if this was a common occurrence or just my plain bad luck. I searched and searched but could find nothing on the subject. Then, while researching another story recently, I came across a series of studies on Murphy's Law, and one of them just happened to be on the checkout line problem.

Let me just sidetrack for a second and tell you a little bit about Murphy's Law. It is generally stated as "Anything that can go wrong, will go wrong." In reality, Murphy never said these words, but they are a good generalization of his original statement.

Believe it or not, Edward A. Murphy was a real man who lived from 1917 to 1990. During the late 1940s, Murphy, an engineer, was involved in a military project to test the effects of rapid deceleration (negative acceleration) on the human body. You have probably seen these tests in old History Channel footage. They strap some poor living subject into a chair, attach a rocket to the chair, and shoot him off at a very high speed. (And you wonder why they call them test *dummies???*)

*Boom!* The guy goes zooming down the track. . . .

(According to Newton's first law of motion, an object at rest will remain at rest. As a result, once the experiment is over, they have to go get the poor guy's stomach back at the starting point.)

Almost instantaneously, the guy is brought to a halt.

*Splat!* It's like hitting a rock wall at top speed.

If the volunteer lives, then the test is a success. If the guy dies, well . . .

On one of these tests in 1949, the test subject was a guy named Captain John Paul Stapp. He was strapped into the chair and exposed to what was thought to be record decelerations. Stapp survived and stumbled out of the chair with bloodshot eyes and bleeding from some of his orifices. When Stapp inquired about how many g's he had been subject to, the response was a big fat zero. Stapp had suffered all of that pain for nothing.

Huh? How could that be?

The designer of the rocket's harness called in Murphy to take a look at the apparatus. What he found would be of no surprise to anyone that knows of his law today. Yes, all sixteen of the sensor electrodes attached to the harness had been wired backward. This led Murphy to state, "If there are two or more ways of doing something, and one of them can lead to catastrophe, then someone will do it." That is the true statement of Murphy's Law, although it has evolved into the simple phrase that we use today.

In regards to the checkout line, Murphy's Law should be restated as, "No matter which line I choose, I will be the last to leave the store." At least it seems that way. A British research scientist named Robert Matthews has been studying various examples of Murphy's Law since 1994, and he did actually study the checkout lines at the store. His scenario was a little simpler than my real-life experiences. Let's suppose you get to the checkout and there are three identical lines to choose from. All of them have the same number of customers, the same number and assortment of groceries, and the same skilled cashier. (Like that could ever happen . . .) You choose the middle line because you have a gut feeling that you will get out of the store faster. In reality, you only have a one-in-three chance of being in the fastest line. In my case, my local supermarket typically has five lines open every time I do my weekly shopping, so I have a one-in-five chance of being on the slowest line. No wonder I always seem to be standing there.

Another Murphy's Law study that Matthews has done is in regard to falling toast. (A bagel in my case.) Why is it that when the toast falls, it always seems to land with the buttered side down? I bumped this question off one of my friends the other day, and she gave me the answers that I had expected. First, she said that the toast's chance of falling on one side versus the other was really a fifty-fifty split. When I pointed out that studies clearly show that there is a tendency to land buttered side down, she then stated that it must have something to do with gravity. You know, the buttered side is heavier, so gravity pulls it down first. Wrong-o, I pointed out. Newton clearly demonstrated that all objects accelerate to the ground at the same rate, regardless of mass.

The real reason that the toast lands buttered side down has to do with the height of people, which in turn places all tables at around the same distance above the floor. It is fairly safe to assume that the toast is on the plate buttered side up and that it basically slides horizontally off the table. And, as we have all observed, the toast will start to spin along its journey to the floor. This spin is something that is known to us science geeks as *torque*. The toast naturally starts to spin, but because of the height of the table, it does not have enough time to return to butter-up position before hitting the ground. Matthews's study concludes that in order for the toast to flip right side up, the table would have to be placed at a height of 3 meters (approximately 10 feet) off the ground, or the size of the toast would have to be reduced to 2.5 centimeters (around one inch). (In other words, the Jolly Green Giant would have to knock a piece of Niblet's toast off the table.)

Murphy's Law also applies to maps. Did you ever notice that when you try to look up a destination on a map, it always seems to be along one of the edges or folds? And since most people are inept at folding maps, this is a significant problem. Again, researcher Matthews comes to us with an explanation. He was able to show, using simple geometry, that 50 percent of the area of a typical road map actually lies in the outer 10 percent perimeter. In other words, there is a very good chance that the place that you are looking for is along the map edge or a fold in an area that he refers to as "the Murphy Zone."

Matthews has studied other instances of Murphy's Law, like "Carrying an umbrella makes forecasted rain less likely to fall" (not true), "If odd socks can be created, they will" (true), and "Cars always break down on the way to important meetings" (not true).

Which leads me to my favorite example of Murphy's Law. In the early 1980s, the Soviet Union decided to send space probes to Venus to explore its surface. In case you didn't know, Venus is a planet covered in dense clouds of carbon dioxide and is suffering from the runaway greenhouse effect. If we burn enough fossil fuels, we could end up living in a place just like it. The planet is just so unbearably hot that all of the space probes sent there are believed to have melted within a few hours of arrival. The first two *Venera* probes that the Soviets sent were supposed to take photographs of the surface. Unfortunately, none were taken. Why? Scientists concluded that the lens caps melted from the intense heat. Improvements were made and in 1982, two more *Venera* probes were sent. A new mechanism was fitted onto the camera to pop the lens cap off before it succumbed to the heat. Each craft was also equipped with a spring-loaded plunger that was designed to measure the compressibility of the Venusian surface. Since the spring was compressed while back on earth, the test could be done only once. *Venera 13* popped the lens cap off and sampled the soil's compressibility without a hitch. *Venera 14* was not as lucky. The lens cap popped right off, but Murphy's Law kicked right in. It landed right under the sampling plunger. The spring went off and hit the lens cap. Yes, the Soviet space probe had traveled through the vast expanse of space just to sample the lens cap that was made back here on earth.

It figures. . . .

Useless? Useful? I'll leave that for you to decide.

# arbor day

## a forgotten tradition

When I first started teaching at my current school district, all I kept hearing from everyone was that the kids shut down after Arbor Day. My first reaction was "Arbor what???" Maybe your reaction is the same. So, if you happen to be in the same boat as I once was, I will explain a little bit about Arbor Day and why it signals the end of our school year.

Arbor Day was the brainchild of a guy named J. Sterling Morton. The *J* stood for Julius, but he was always known as Sterling. You may not have ever heard of him, but you have surely heard of the company called Morton Salt that one of his son's owned, which many years later became Morton Thiokol and took most of the blame for the Space Shuttle *Challenger* disaster. Born in Adams, New York, on April 22, 1832, and raised in Monroe, Michigan, J. Sterling Morton headed west in 1854 to the largely unsettled Nebraska Territory. Within a year of his arrival, he assumed the role of editor of the *Nebraska City News* and built a large home on a 160-acre piece of land. His house was considered a mansion in its day but upon completion it lacked two important details: trees and green plants. Yes, it was 160 acres of basically nothing.

It was widely assumed at the time that the land was not well suited for farming or for growing trees, but that didn't stop Morton and his wife. Trees, shrubs, and flowers were planted all around the property, and they grew quickly. Using his mighty pen, Morton spread his word of planting trees to his readers. He encouraged others to do the same. Not only did the trees offer beauty, but they also were an excellent way to block the high winds that blew across the plains, provided wood for fuel and construction, and blocked out the intense rays of that mighty yellow thing in the sky.

Morton entered the world of politics and was eventually appointed by President Buchanan as the secretary and acting governor of the Nebraska Territory. He later lost a bid to be elected the state's first governor, so he turned his head toward his true passion of promoting agriculture. One of Morton's major goals was the establishment of a day set aside statewide each year for the planting of trees.

The new holiday, which was first celebrated on April 10, 1872, was called . . . drum roll, please . . . Arbor Day. Now, if you are a complete dodo like me, you are probably wondering who Arbor was and why anyone would name a tree-planting holiday after him. Joseph P. Arbor was . . . No, not really. As I soon learned, Arbor was not a person but a word derived from the Latin term for "tree." Duh! I should have known. Arbor Day basically means Tree Day. It couldn't get any simpler than that.

Today, we seem to have holidays for just about everything. Secretary's Day, Grandparents Day, Eat Toxic Lead Paint Day . . . Hey, there is even serious consideration of making my birthday a national holiday. (Serious consideration by me.) So, one would think that Arbor Day would have just been another reason for Hallmark to sell cards. I learned, to my amazement, that when the first Arbor Day was celebrated, over 1 million trees were planted in the state of Nebraska. Within sixteen years, a total of 350 million trees had been planted. While the state is well populated today, just how many people could there have been living in Nebraska way back then? I was thinking something like four people. (It was really a little less than 500,000 people.) They had to do some serious planting to stick all of those trees into the ground.

Of course, the politicians quickly smelled something good to latch onto and in 1885, Arbor Day was signed into law in Nebraska.

The date was changed to April 22, in honor of J. Sterling Morton's birthday.

Yet, with all of this success, Morton never pushed for Arbor Day beyond his own state. That took the work of a conservationist named Birdsey Norton. He decided to spread the gospel of Arbor Day and encouraged that it become part of every child's education. Within ten years of the first Arbor Day, schools all around the United States were celebrating this day with parades, music, recitations, tree dedications, and, of course, tree plantings.

Which leads us back to Chatham, New York, and the school where I teach. Right after Governor David B. Hill signed Arbor Day into law in 1889, celebrations were held all over New York State. Our community was no exception. That very year, our school planted its very first tree and dedicated it to the one and only Steve Silverman. Oops, I mean George Washington. George's tree no longer stands, so one can only assume that it suffered a fate similar to that of the famous cherry tree. There are only so many Washingtons, so in 1900 the decision was made to dedicate future Arbor Day trees to people that had had a major impact on education in our community. Today, Chatham has the oldest Arbor Day tree in New York State. It's an oak tree that was dedicated by the class of 1902 to a Miss Harriet Seymour. Not that anyone recalls who she actually was.

In case you haven't noticed, Arbor Day has basically disappeared from the American holiday landscape. The holiday had been so successful initially that most of the country's depleted forests had been replenished. With the growing use of cars in the early twentieth century, the U.S. government started promoting something called Good Roads Arbor Day, which essentially had the unwritten goal of paving over the American landscape. (Hidden meaning: Chop down 10,000 trees for this new road and plant one new one over there.) This and many other factors led to the demise of Arbor Day.

Even in Chatham, where Arbor Day is still celebrated each year, the day has been watered down to basically nothing. Different district administrators have tried unsuccessfully to get the day wiped off the calendar. What was once an entire week of activities, contests, and celebration has now been reduced to one 24-hour period at the end of May. Our Arbor Day celebration is broken down into four basic segments:

1. *Arbor Day Banquet.* A free meal hosted by the junior class. (Free??? Did someone say free??? You can be sure that I'm there.)

2. *Senior Prank.* Students sneak into the school overnight and leave something original to remember them by. The best one I have ever witnessed was when the students removed the giant C, T, and M from the first word of the school sign outside. Instead of reading CHATHAM HIGH SCHOOL, it now read HA HA HIGH SCHOOL That's originality, if you ask me.

3. *Tree-Planting Ceremony.* Forty-five minutes of typical boring speeches, dedications, acceptances, and other blah-blah. Then, all of the seniors and teachers are given small shovels to scoop dirt back into the hole that the new tree has been planted in.

4. *Arbor Day Games.* Pack 400 screaming kids into a small gym and you will know what the meaning of loud really is.

And then our Arbor Day celebration is over. The kids decide that they are done for the year. All learning comes to an abrupt halt, even though a month still remains of school.

So, if you are one of those people looking to restore some tradition to America's schools, why don't you propose that your district celebrate Arbor Day? My wisecracks aside, it really is a wonderful day to celebrate. Start out small and let the celebration grow over the years, just like the trees. And, let's face it, there's nothing wrong with planting a few trees and having a good time.

Useless? Useful? I'll leave that for you to decide.

J. Sterling Morton, the founder of Arbor Day. Photo was signed on New Year's Day, 1895. (Library of Congress)

# the electric pickle

## let's hear it for pickle power!

Several years ago, I had a student named Daegan who kept bugging me with the same comment every time that I did a demonstration for the class. Basically, he kept telling me that he would not be happy until I set my tie on fire. After months of hearing this comment repeated, I finally decided to make his wish come true. I designed a demonstration in which I took my ugliest tie, soaked it in rubbing alcohol, and then set it ablaze. Daegan was not impressed, however, because the tie was still intact after the fire went out. He wanted the tie to be burned to a crisp. I, on the other hand, wanted to teach some science. (As I tell all my students, please do not try this at home!)

Obviously, there was some sort of deception going on with my tie experiment. Let's just say, without revealing my secret, that the alcohol was not what it appeared to be. The tie trick did, however, lead me to the one demonstration that my students seem to remember for life. It, too, has a bit of magic to it. And, because it involves something known as a *suicide plug,* I am not going to tell you exactly how to do it. In other words, don't try this one at home, either.

Every school year, my last demo is always what my students refer to as the "electrocution of a pickle." Basically, this works on a principle very similar to that of frying someone in an electric chair. Just put a current through something juicy that conducts electricity and watch it sizzle.

What is unusual about the pickle is that is doesn't just cook. Within a short period of time, steam starts to escape out the sides and, amazingly, it starts to light up like a lightbulb. Yes, you read that correctly. It emits light. Yellow light, to be specific. And the smell . . . Let's just say that the word *bad* does not describe the odor well enough!

Now, I would be lying if I told you that I came up with this trick on my own. I didn't. In fact, I first saw it demonstrated at a physics teacher training course that I was taking back in 1991. I was captivated by what I was watching and knew that my students would be equally fascinated. That night I went home and built my own apparatus to perform the demo. Unfortunately, our school principal did not approve of the idea (can anybody say, "Lawsuit"???) and forbade me from doing the demo for a couple of years. When a newly hired teacher down the hall from me started doing it, followed by Mr. Wizard performing the electrocution on the Nickelodeon channel, I convinced the administration to let me do it.

What amazes me most about this demo is that no one ever explained to me what it was supposed to prove. It just looked cool. Who cared if the glowing pickle really ever taught any concept? Again, it just looked cool! Well, I quickly found out that my students really did care.

They thought that they had finally stumped me, but they hadn't. Every good teacher learns that they must be ready for anything, and I was. I gave them some cockamamy story about how it all tied into Niels Bohr's model of the atom. It seemed to me that the electricity flowing into the pickle excited the electrons in the sodium ions that made up the pickle's salt content. When the electrons fell back down to a stable orbital, the yellow light was emitted. It all made perfect sense to me because I remembered doing flame tests in college chemistry in which sodium emitted a similar yellow light.

In plain English, this means that you add energy to throw something up and then you get the energy back when it comes back down. To prove this, just take a rock and throw it straight up in the air. You have to add energy to throw the rock upward. When it comes down and hits you on the head, you will quickly realize that it just transferred that energy back to you.

Honestly, this did not take much thought on my part to figure out. It just seemed fairly obvious to me. Well, it turns out that scientists have been working feverishly to solve the mystery of the glowing pickle.

I recently learned that two important (yeah, right!) papers have been published on the topic.

Seven researchers at Digital Computers did the first study in April 1989. Their findings were just amazing. They concluded that kosher dill pickles were the best because they had the highest salt content. Also, they determined that pickles would not make good lightbulbs because they only gave off yellow light and they smelled really, really bad. Duh! They published their results in a paper titled "Characterization of Organic Illumination Systems." There is nothing as effective as using big words in a publication title so that no one can understand it. Its April 1 publication date should give a big hint as to how serious they considered this study to be.

The second set of findings was released by a team of four scientists in 1993 and appeared in the *Journal of Chemical Education.* Their findings? Very simple. The light emitted by the pickle was nearly identical to that released by the sodium atom. Just as I had suspected.

Don't get me wrong. I am not trying to diminish the need for serious scientific studies. Yet, I can't help but get a small chuckle when I see how much time and energy goes into these projects. I have a hunch that they were also laughing while writing these studies up. Sometimes there is a need for making science fun and interesting, even if it proves very little.

Useless? Useful? I'll leave that for you to decide.

# hiroo onoda

## hey! the war is over!

One of the hot topics that is discussed in my physics classroom every year has to do with space travel. According to Einstein's theory, as one approaches the speed of light, time slows down. What this means is that you could theoretically get into a spaceship, travel near the speed of light for a year or two, and then return. You will have aged very little. Yet, everyone back here on our mighty blue planet will have aged considerably more. Upon your return, you would also find that the earth's technology, politics, and economics would have changed dramatically. Life would have changed so much that you would no longer fit in.

In one sense, this is exactly what happened to a man named Hiroo Onoda. For thirty years, Onoda was stuck in that time warp known as 1944. The rest of the world continued to change around him, but Onoda stayed the same. When he reemerged into our modern world, he was not prepared for what he saw. Onoda, of course, never did travel into space. Instead, he was lost in another form of time.

How Onoda ended up in this situation can really be traced back to his youth. He was born in Kainan, Japan, in 1922, and when he turned seventeen, he went to work for a trading company in China. Onoda lived the life of any ordinary teenager. He worked all day and partied all night at the local dance halls.

In May 1942, Onoda was drafted into the Japanese military right after the United States entered the war and fighting escalated to a global scale. Unlike most soldiers, he attended a school that trained men for guerrilla warfare. At a time when becoming a prisoner of war was considered by the Japanese to be a crime punishable by death, Onoda was taught to stay alive at all costs.

On December 26, 1944, Apprentice Officer Hiroo Onoda was sent to the small tropical island of Lubang, which is approximately seventy-five miles southwest of Manila in the Philippines. His orders were straightforward. He was to do anything to hamper enemy attack on the island. This included destroying the Lubang airport and the pier at the harbor. He was sent in alone, ordered not to die by his own hand, and told to take as many years as was needed to accomplish his mission.

When Onoda landed on the island, he met up with a group of Japanese soldiers that had been sent there previously. The officers in this group outranked Private Onoda and prevented him from carrying out his assignment in a timely manner. This just made it all that much easier for the Americans to take control of the island when they landed on February 28. Within a short period of time, all but Onoda and three of the other Japanese soldiers had either died or surrendered. Onoda, having just been promoted to lieutenant, ordered the men to take to the hills. The war ended shortly thereafter, but the four soldiers would not know it for quite some time.

Let's face reality here. Four surviving soldiers cannot fight much of a war. Basically, they can only fight for their survival. Realizing that it would be unwise to stay in any one location for a long period of time, they developed a circuit, of sorts, in which they moved from point to point. A long stay in any particular place would be three to five days, the length of time determined mainly by the supply of food. During the torrential rains of the monsoon season, no one came into the mountains, and they were able to build a camp and sit still for a longer duration.

Their main source of nourishment was bananas. Now, I don't know about you, but one or two bananas are just fine, but having them as my dinner every day would not be something that I would look forward to. Of course, they had to sustain their health somehow. They did supplement their diet by eating other fruits and by hunting water buffalo, wild boar, wild chickens, and iguanas. (Mmm, mmm, good . . .) They preferred beef, but they could not hunt too many of any animal because the sound of their gunshots would quickly indicate their position.

## And Then There Were Three

The first of the four to go was Private First Class Yuichi Akatsu. He got fed up with the whole thing and stormed off in September 1949. The remaining men figured that there was no way that this weakling could survive on his own. Yet, unbeknownst to them, Akatsu managed to live six months on his own before surrendering to the Philippine Army. In 1950, the remaining three found a note left by Akatsu stating that he had been greeted by friendly American troops. He had even led a group of soldiers into the mountains in search of the remaining men. Onoda and his men quickly concluded that Akatsu was now working with the enemy and retreated to the other side of the mountain.

In 1952, letters and photographs of family and friends were dropped all over the island from an airplane. The soldiers concluded that the enemy had finally outdone themselves with this clever trick. To the eye of those trained in guerrilla warfare, this had to be a hoax.

## And Another One Gone

In June 1953, Corporal Shimada, another member of their party, was shot in the leg during a shoot-out with some fishermen. Onoda nursed him back to health, but on May 7, 1954, Shimada was killed instantly from a shot fired by another search party sent in to find the men.

Ten days later, more leaflets were dropped. A loudspeaker blurted out, "Onoda, Kozuka, the war has ended." Clearly, this was another trick by the Americans. They were sure that the war was still on, and they intended to get even with the enemy for Shimada's death. Onoda and Kozuka were positive that the Japanese would be landing on the island any day and that control would be taken back from the Americans.

One day, Onoda's own brother stood by at the microphone and

pleaded for them to give up. Onoda could not see the speaker's face from his great distance and concluded that the Americans had gone to a really great length to trick him this time. They believed that the Americans had found a man that was built and sounded just like his brother but was really an imposter!

You must understand their whole rationale. First, they were trained to treat everything with suspicion. Second, it was well understood that it could take 100 years to win the war and that Japan would never surrender until every last Japanese citizen had been killed. In their minds, there were still Japanese citizens alive, so, clearly, the war must still be going on.

Whenever they needed crucial supplies, the two men would "requisition" them from the islanders. You and I would call it armed robbery, but since this was considered a time of war, these actions were considered acceptable. The islanders had several names for them, including "mountain bandits" and "mountain devils." The islanders had good reason to fear them, since many of the island's citizens had been wounded or killed in skirmishes with the two soldiers.

In late 1965, Onoda and Kozuka requisitioned a transistor radio and listened to reports from Peking. Oddly, with their minds still trapped in wartime 1945, they did not believe anything that they heard on the radio regarding military or foreign relations. Yet, they followed the horse races and understood that Japan had risen to be a great industrial power.

**The Last Man Standing**

Each year, in an effort to continue on with their military assignment, Onoda and Kozuka would burn piles of rice that had been collected by the farmers. On October 19, 1972, they went about their usual business but decided to burn one last small rice pile before they went on their way. This was a big mistake. This gave the police ample time to get there and they shot Kozuka twice. One of the bullets went through his heart, and he was killed.

Onoda took to the woods once again. He resolved that if he encountered the enemy, he would shoot to kill. The loudspeaker announcements and the dropping of leaflets intensified. Search parties left magazines and newspapers behind, many detailing the incredible funeral that was held for Kozuka back in Japan. Yet, to no one's surprise, Onoda did not buy their pleas.

For almost one more year, Onoda continued to live on his own. He was prepared to die on the island. Then, on February 20, 1974, he encountered a young Japanese university dropout named Suzuki living alone in a tent. Suzuki had left Japan to travel the world and told his friends that he was "going to look for Lieutenant Onoda, a panda, and the Abominable Snowman," in that order. (We know he found Onoda; he could go to any big zoo to see a panda; but one can't help but wonder if he ever found the Abominable Snowman.) Onoda approached cautiously and the two soon struck up a conversation that lasted many hours. The two became friends, but Onoda said that he couldn't leave with Suzuki because he was awaiting orders from one of his commanders.

Suzuki left and promised that he would return. And he did.

On March 9, 1974, Onoda went to an agreed-upon location and found a note that had been left by Suzuki. Along with the note, Suzuki had enclosed two photos that they had taken together the first time that they met, along with copies of two Army orders. The next day, Onoda decided to take a chance and made a two-day journey to meet up with Suzuki. His long hike paid off handsomely. Suzuki had brought along Onoda's one-time superior commander, Major Taniguchi, who delivered the oral orders for Onoda to surrender his sword.

Hiroo Onoda's thirty-year war was now over. He returned to Japan to receive a hero's welcome. He was a media sensation and was hounded by the curious public everywhere he went.

Yet, Onoda's mind was still living in 1944 Japan, and he had a strong dislike for what he now saw. After publishing his memoirs, he took his newly found fortune and moved to Brazil to raise cattle. He then married a Japanese woman and moved back to Japan to run a nature camp for kids, which he still operates today. (We can be quite sure that he had a lot of expertise about nature.)

Useless? Useful? I'll leave that for you to decide.

# rubber duckies

## the quack heard around the world

Perhaps you were one of the millions of people that went to see the movie *The Perfect Storm*. Whether you were there to drool over George Clooney or for the great special effects, you probably took little notice of the one scene that stood out in my mind. It was of a giant freighter that was being tossed about by the great waves and lost its cargo to the ocean floor. My mind instantly said, *Rubber duckies*. It was immediately followed by the thought of Nike sneakers. I'll bet that your mind was thinking of something else.

What I am talking about here is known as flotsam. Having never lived by the ocean, I had to check with my longtime friend Mr. Webster to find out what the term actually meant. Let's just say that it's all of the junk that is floating around in our oceans from the ever-perilous doings of mankind. Like me, I think that you will be amazed by the stuff that is finding its way onto the shores of the earth's coastlines.

The message-in-a-bottle idea seems as old as time itself. You know, you somehow end up stranded alone on a deserted island. You lose all your worldly possessions except for a glass bottle, a pencil, and a piece of paper. You proceed to scribble a cry of desperation on the paper and seal it in the bottle, and after you die, someone actually finds it washed up on some distant beach.

Yet, bottles are not the only things washing up on our beaches. It is estimated that at least 1,000 shipping containers are washed overboard from ships crossing the various oceans every year. When I say containers, I am not talking about those little Tupperware containers in which you store your perishable foods; I am talking *big*.

Actually, *huge* may be a better term. Each one of these shipping containers measures approximately forty feet long and is the size of your typical boxcar. And, of course, big containers hold lots of stuff.

Take, for example, the accident that occurred in the North Pacific at 48°N, 161°W on May 27, 1990. The ship *Hansa Carrier* encountered some really rough weather while on its journey from Korea to the United States. The winds and the waves tossed the ship around like it was a toy boat in a bathtub. Some of the strappings holding its cargo to the deck snapped and sent twenty-one of its shipping containers to the ocean floor. It was later learned that five of these containers contained about 80,000 Nike athletic shoes of various types. Although no one knows for sure, it is estimated that about 61,000 Nike shoes were sent adrift. Six months later, the shoes started showing up along the beaches of Vancouver and the states of Washington and Oregon. Overall, there were documented reports of about 1,300 of the shoes floating ashore. Because of their different profiles, it was not uncommon for the wind to carry left shoes to one beach and rights to another.

If there was anything man-made that was meant to be washed overboard, it was certainly our next product. On January 10, 1992, another ship left Hong Kong for Puget Sound. Right near the international date line, it ran into the same trouble as the last ship. But, in this case, one of the cargo containers that washed overboard contained 29,000 children's bathtub toys called floaties. More specifically, there was now an armada of yellow rubber duckies, red beavers, blue turtles, and green frogs sailing the ocean blue. Their first cry had to be "Freedom at last!" when they escaped from their plastic and cardboard packaging prisons. Hundreds of them eventually washed up on the west coast of North America. Yet, there are a countless number of them still floating around the Pacific and enjoying the view.

Coming in as a close second to the rubber duckies in terms of appropriateness has to be the great loss of 4,756,940 Lego parts that spilled off the *Tokio Express* on February 13, 1997, about twenty miles off the coast of Land's End, England. Oddly, these were not your typical Lego blocks. Instead, this spill contained pieces that seemed destined for the brink. It included divers, pirates, octopuses, life preservers, and yellow life rafts, all headed for the United States to be included in toy kits depicting sea adventures. And, boy did they have a sea adventure! Of the approximately 100 styles of Lego parts dumped into the sea, 53 of them were capable of floating. Within days, Lego pieces started washing up on Cornwall's shores.

Another interesting spill occurred on December 9, 1994, while the *Hyundai Seattle* was making its way from Korea to a Seattle port. Like the others, the ship was knocked around by mountainous waves, and forty-nine containers fell overboard. Sent to Davy Jones's locker were piles of Spiderman and Power Ranger toys, more athletic shoes, black beach sandals, and other things. Of most interest to the public at the time were the 34,000 hockey gloves and the other hockey gear that eventually made its way to the beaches of the Pacific Northwest. (One could earn some extra pocket cash collecting stuff from these beaches.)

The list of items unintentionally dumped into the sea goes on and on. The *Pol American* lost twenty-three containers on March 31, 1997, off the coast of Cape Cod. Nantucket beachcombers found sealed bags of Hershey's Kisses, Tootsie Rolls, and other delectable goodies washed up along their shore. A Chinese cargo ship headed for Hong Kong lost 500,000 cans of beer. (Someone was surely screaming, "Party!") In January 1997, another ship lost 100,000 toy cars and 1 million party balloons to the sea. Hundreds of flip-flops washed up on Australian beaches from another accident. The *APL China* sent somewhere between 366 and 406 containers overboard in October 1999 loaded with furniture, televisions, clothing, and who knows what else.

As fascinating as all this may seem to collectors of this junk and to the average reader, it is not the bed of roses that it appears to be. Take, for instance, the near disaster that occurred on January 4,

1992, right off the coast of New Jersey. The *Santa Clara I* was headed from New York to Baltimore when twenty-one of its containers were thrown overboard. Most of them were empty or contained harmless materials, but four of them held arsenic trioxide. Just the word *arsenic* should send shivers down your spine. Basically, this stuff is used to make rat poison, insecticides, and herbicides, and is used as a wood preservative. In other words, it is a deadly poison. Four hundred fourteen 25-gallon drums fell into the sea. According to federal officials, that is enough to make approximately 170 million aspirin-sized tablets and would be capable of killing one-half of the U.S. population.

What to do? What to do?

Believe it or not, the spill was not immediately reported. And once it was, it took a while to find the containers. Three were located in 120 feet of water and the fourth was believed to have dropped its load nearby. Some of the drums had actually imploded from the water pressure. Robots were used to move the drums into larger fifty-five-gallon drums, which were then lifted to the surface. The Food and Drug Administration tested clams and scallops from the area for arsenic contamination, but only normal background levels were recorded. In the end, the effects were minimal, but we almost didn't get away that luckily.

What this basically points out is that while the thought of having rubber duckies, Nike sneakers, Lego parts, and bags of candy floating up on the shoreline makes for some interesting conversations, the reality is that this is nothing but pure pollution.

Yet, what appears as pollution and garbage to one person could be of great worth to another. Take the case of Dr. Curtis C. Ebbesmeyer, an oceanographer in Seattle, Washington. His life changed back in 1991 when his mother read about all of those Nike shoes mysteriously washing up on the Pacific beaches. Up to this point, he had followed the ocean's currents using special drifters that were tracked by satellites. He quickly realized that there were tens of thousands of shoes drifting their way across the Pacific that could be used to gain similar information. In collaboration with W. James

Ingraham Jr. of the National Marine Fisheries Service, he was able to use the computer program OSCURS (short for *Ocean Surface CURrent Simulations*) to plot the path of the sneakers over time. He did the same for the rubber ducky, hockey glove, and other future spills. And, believe it or not, his predictions were typically right on the money. By collecting the data on these drifting objects, OSCURS will, over time, be able to predict where potentially dangerous spills, such as those from oil and chemical disasters, will wash ashore.

One of those rubber duckies could just save someone's life. And to think that it could be yours.

Useless? Useful? I'll leave that for you to decide.

# references

The major sources used in writing this book are described below. Each set of references is broken down into the two categories of "Web Links" and "Print Media and Additional Resources." Please be aware that Web pages come and go and are rarely, if ever, updated. While the quality and quantity of research information on the Web has improved over the past several years, I would still use caution when using any Web page as a primary source. Anyone can pretend to be an expert on the Internet. The "Print Media and Additional Resources" category, on the other hand, is typically more reliable. It includes books, magazine and newspaper articles, television shows, and any other medium that may have been useful.

Unlike those of most written works, the references here are not listed in order by author or date. Instead, I have chosen to list them in their general order of importance. References at the top of each section are, based on my experience, the best places to start your research. Those at the bottom are typically shorter in length and of less value to a researcher.

As in the previous volume, *Einstein's Refrigerator,* I have chosen to use the SSS, or the *Steve Silverman style,* for listing sources. I have avoided the MLA or a similar citation style so that I could personalize each source. Several English teachers have tried to correct my unusual method, but it is what works best for this type of book. My rationale for this unusual method of citation is that I have been sorely disappointed by the citations listed in many other works. Their formal styles of citation tend to give every reference equal importance, yet that can never be true. I cannot begin to tell you how many times I have spent hours hunting down a particular source only to be sorely disappointed in what it had to offer. I am hoping that the SSS, my plain-English method of citing works, will be of great help to those that wish to do further research on these topics.

# Part 1: Uh, Oh!

## THE FLUBBER FIASCO
**Web Links**

There are many minor blurbs about this incident on the Web. One of the more complete ones is "Great Moments in Toy Marketing: Flubber" in *Stay Free!* magazine *(http://www.stayfreemagazine.org/archives/13/flubber.html)*. This gives a nice overview of the story, but exploring the resources of a good library may be a better place to start.

**Print Media and Additional Resources**

One of the more interesting articles available is "The Flubber That Wouldn't Die" by Bernard Reich. Appearing originally in the *Jerusalem Post* (November 7, 1997, page 6), Reich's story differs quite a bit from other sources available. However, since he was the man placed in charge of disposing of the Flubber, one can safely assume that Reich knows exactly what he is talking about.

Author G. Wayne Miller has included the Flubber story in *Toy Wars: The Epic Struggle Between G.I. Joe, Barbie, and the Companies That Make Them* (1998, Times Books, New York, pages 24–26).

A short summary can be found in the December 15, 1997, *Time* magazine story "Flubber: the Toy, the Sequel," which is located at the bottom of page 41.

## THE GREAT TOILET PAPER SHORTAGE
**Web Links**

There are numerous brief mentions of this topic on the Web. Take a look at "How Funny Is Toilet Paper?" on the How2 Web site.

It offers a little more detail than most of the other sources (*http://www.how2.co.uk/how/120307.html*).

**Print Media and Additional Resources**

The history of toilet paper and the associated statistics come from the very unusual book *RE/Search Guide to Bodily Fluids* by Paul Spinrad. It is published by RE/Search publications (San Francisco, Calif., 1994).

The book *Uncle John's Bathroom Reader* by the Bathroom Readers' Institute (1995, The Bathroom Readers' Press, Berkeley, Calif., pages 217–218) offers up the story "The Great Toilet Paper Shortage." It's actually a reprint of a *TV Guide* article from 1974.

The *New York Times* has two articles on this story:

- "Toilet Paper Scant in Washington Area" (June 3, 1974, page 22, column 1)
- "Scott Company Rationing Toilet Paper on East Coast" (June 13, 1974, page 44, column 4)

"FIGHT!"

**Print Media and Additional Resources**

A short summary of this story can be found on page 100 of the book *The Twentieth Century* by David Wallechinsky (1995, Little, Brown and Company, New York).

An excellent report on this incident can be found in the article titled "Seventy-Eight Negroes Killed in a Mad Panic" from the Saturday, September 20, 1902, issue of the *New York Times* (page 1). This story is a very detailed preliminary report on the events that occurred.

THE EXPLODING WHALE

**Web Links**

This is a story that can be found in various forms all over the Internet. Using your search engine of choice, you should have no problem hunting down information on this story.

Dave DeBry's 1996 Web page, "The Infamous Exploding Whale," is one of the most popular pages out there on the subject *(http://www.perp.com/whale/)*. The site features video snapshots and links to the actual video of the news report.

A classic among urban folklore enthusiasts, a great discussion of the event can be found on the Urban Legends Reference Pages site. "The Exploded Whale" *(http://www.snopes.com/critters/disposal/whale.htm)* confirms that it is a true story and offers up a conversation between the author and Ed Schoaps, the public affairs coordinator for the Oregon Department of Transportation.

Go to Hackstadt.com for Steve Hackstadt's transcription of the famous 1970 news segment featuring Paul Linnman of KATU and, of course, the whale *(http://www.hackstadt.com/features/whale/transcript)*.

**Print Media and Additional Resources**

There is an excellent article by Larry Bacon titled "Beached Whale: Thar She Blows," which ran in the November 12, 1995, issue of the *Register-Guard* (section B, pages 1 and 2).

The *Washington Post* ran a short UPI story on the whale: "Forty Tons of Blubber Are Sent Flying" (November 14, 1970, page A9, column 6).

The *New York Times* offers up the paragraph "Dead Whale ls Dynamited" (November 15, 1970, page 62, column 6). Also based on the UPI wire feed, the shorter *New York Times* version suggests they did not expect this to be a story that hung around for a long time.


THE PESHTIGO FIRE
Web Links

One of the best on-line sources is the book *The Great Peshtigo Fire: An Eyewitness Account* by Father Peter Pernin, who survived the disastrous fire. This 1874 book has been reprinted and can be purchased at your local bookstore. The entire text of Father Pernin's book has also been placed on the Wisconsin Electronic Reader Web site *(http://www.library.wisc.edu/etext/wireader/WER2002-1.html)*.

On the same Web site, there is a reprint of the Wisconsin Academy Review article, "The Great Fires of 1871 in the Northwest," by Professor I. A. Lapham in 1965 *(http://www.library.wisc.edu/etext/wireader/WER0133.html)*.

Deana C. Hipke has prepared "The Great Peshtigo Fire of 1871" (1999), which details the fire and offers an excellent listing of references, to further your research on the topic *(http://www.peshtigofire.info/)*.

**Print Media and Additional Resources**

While not one of the most interesting of books to read, Robert W. Wells has written a very thorough accounting of the Peshtigo disaster titled *Fire at Peshtigo* (1968, Prentice-Hall, Englewood Cliffs, N.J.).

The October 1996 issue of *American Heritage* (volume 47, issue 6, page 118) contains Frederic D. Schwarz's article "1871: One Hundred and Twenty-Five Years Ago." At only six paragraphs, it is fairly short but offers useful information.

Try to locate the transcript of NPR's October 7, 2000, broadcast of *All Things Considered,* in which Wisconsin Public Radio's Patty Murray profiles the "deadliest forest fire in America" with the help of two experts.


THE HORRORS OF DHMO

Web Links

There are a number of sites on the Internet devoted to DHMO. The easiest place to start is in the "Humor" directory of Yahoo *(http://dir.yahoo.com/Entertainment/Humor/Science/Chemistry_Humor/Dihydrogen_Monoxide/)*.

Be sure to check out the Dihydrogen Monoxide Research Division Web site at *http://www.dhmo.org/*. It has a very official, governmental look to it.

# Part 2: The Creative Mind at Work

THE MATCHSTICK MAN

Web Links

The most complete story on Jack's collection can be found on The Cutlery Collection *(http://www.thecutlerycollection.com/*

*main.htm)* Web site. Titled "Matchstick Madness," this story offers a nice summary of Jack's hobby as well as some great photographs.

Jantje Blokhuis-Mulder has written the excellent story "Jack Hall: The Matchstick Man" *(http://www.jantjeblokhuismulder.com/ articles/jackhall.shtml)*.

A special thanks to Jack's son Tony Hall for all of his help in writing this story. All of the photographs accompanying this story on my Web site, as well as the one in this book, have been generously provided by Tony. You can contact him at *tony_hall@lineone.net* for additional information and permissions.

## EVEREADY BATTERIES
### Web Links
Daniel M. Dumych has written an excellent on-line biography, "Joshua Lionel Cowen," located at American National Biography Online *(http://www.anb.org/articles/13/13-00354.html,* December 2001), which is available only by subscription.
### Print Media and Additional Resources
I first came across the story "The Little Engines That Could" by Richard Sassaman on page 64 of the winter 1995 issue of *American Heritage of Invention and Technology.*

Be sure to check out *All Aboard! The Story of Joshua Lionel Cowen and His Lionel Train Company* by Ron Hollander (1981, Workman Publishing Company, New York, pages 21–29). This is the definitive book on Cowen and the history of Lionel trains.

A summary of Lionel trains' history can be found in the October 19, 1952, issue of the *New York Times* (section 3, page 3). The article is titled "Along the Highways and Byways of Finance" and is written by Robert H. Fetridge.

The book *A Toy Is Born* by Marvin Kaye (1973, Stein and Day, New York, pages 27–33) devotes the chapter "Lionel and the American Dream" to Joshua L. Cowen and his trains.

PEZ

Web Links

The Web is loaded with information on PEZ, its origin, and the value of the various dispensers.

Be sure to check out the manufacturer's official site, PEZ.com *(http://www.pez.com)*.

Believe it or not, there is an International PEZ Collectors Association, which can be found at *http://www.pez.org*. This page includes links to additional PEZ sites around the world.

Print Media and Additional Resources

The article "PEZ-o-rama" discusses the history of PEZ. This piece can be found in the May 3, 1993, issue of *Maclean's* on page 13.

Additional information on the history of PEZ can be found in the article "Those Little Candy Pellets Continue to Be Hot Sellers" by Mary Biersdorfer, published by the Gannett News Service on May 26, 1994.

The PEZ watch is described in the article "Technowatch: The Goods: Round-the-Clock Sweetness" by Lynn Simross. This story can be found in the September 16, 1994, issue of the *Los Angeles Times* on page E3.

Finally, if you really need to find out more on the Power PEZ, check out the article "A Whole New Spin on PEZ Circular Dispensers Takes a Modern, Automated Turn" by Katy Kelly (*USA Today*, August 15, 1996, page 1D).

PINK FLAMINGOS

Web Links

"Why Not My Duck?" is a February 25, 1997, interview with pink flamingo creator Don Featherstone. This story appears on the On Stagnant Pond Web site at *http://www.ospsitecrafters.com/ intvwdon.html*.

Print Media and Additional Resources

Perhaps the best reference available is the article "The Plastic Pink Flamingo: A Natural History" by Jennifer Price. Appearing in the spring 1999 *American Scholar* (volume 68, number 2, pages 73–88), this well-written piece will probably provide you with more information than you ever wanted to know about pink flamingos.

Anyone that calls Don Featherstone "my new hero" can't be all that bad. This is how Tim O'Brien refers to Featherstone in his September 15, 1997, *Amusement Business* article "Tim's Place" (volume 109, issue 37, page 4).

"Lawn Art" is a three-page discussion of Featherstone's creation in the book *Plastic: The Making of a Synthetic Century* by Stephen Fenichell (1996, HarperCollins, New York, pages 267–269).

## BARBECUING
**Web Links**

One really doesn't need to look any further than George Goble's Web site for information. Here he has gathered a great collection of articles, photos, audio, and video of his BBQ techniques *(http:// ghg.ecn.purdue.edu/~ghg/)*.

Brief summaries of the history of charcoal briquettes can be found on The Hungover Gourmet *(http://www.hungovergourmet.com/ food/feature/grillarama/grillarama.html)* and on the Kingsford, Michigan, site at *http://www.multimag.com/city/mi/kingsford*.

## LINDBERGH'S ARTIFICIAL HEART
**Web Links**

A quick search of the Web using your favorite search engine will bring up a listing of numerous matches regarding Lindbergh and the artificial heart. Most are limited to one or two paragraphs and are not very useful. One of the better sources is:

"Lindbergh's Heart Pump" by John H. Lienhard on the Engines of Our Ingenuity Web site. Audio of this radio program is also available on this page *(http://www.uh.edu/engines/epi318.htm)*.

**Print Media and Additional Resources**

Probably the best person to tell the story is the inventor himself. *Autobiography of Values* by Charles A. Lindbergh (1977, Harcourt Brace Jovanovich, New York, pages 131–139) has a nice section devoted to Lindbergh's interest in the heart pump. Published shortly after his death, it is interesting to see how some of the minor facts in this story differ from the purported ones that are so commonly tossed around on the Internet.

J. M. Fenster has prepared an excellent story on the development of artificial organs. "The Inner Limits" starts on page 10 of the winter 1998 issue of *American Heritage of Invention and Technology*. The author effectively uses a description of Lindbergh's profusion pump as a jumping-off point for the article.

## PHILO FARNSWORTH
### Web Links
There is certainly no shortage of information on the Internet regarding Farnsworth. Here are some of the sites that I found most useful:

Without a doubt, the best place to start is at *http://www.farnovision.com*. "The Farnsworth Chronicles" by Paul Schatzkin is a well-written, eleven-part history on Farnsworth and his invention. Includes great photographs and additional support materials.

When *Time* magazine named the 100 most important people of the twentieth century, Farnsworth made the list. You can read Neil Postman's March 29, 1999, story at *http://www.time.com/time/time100/scientist/profile/farnsworth.html*.

While I only caught the tail end of the actual show, the transcript for the PBS broadcast of *The American Experience*'s "Big Dream, Small Screen" can be found at *http://www.pbs.org/wgbh/amex/technology/bigdream/bigdreamts.html*.

### Print Media and Additional Resources
The *New York Times* offers the following articles:
- "New Television System: California Inventor Produces Machine to Attach to Radio Sets" (September 4, 1928, page 20, column 1) is a short article that explains that Farnsworth had done away with all of the mechanical parts found in earlier television systems.
- "Tennis Stars Act in New Television" (August 25, 1934, page 14, column 1) discusses the first public demonstration of

television at the Franklin Institute in Philadelphia.

- "Gain in Television Is Demonstrated" (July 31, 1935, page 15, column 4) talks about improvements in Farnsworth's system, including transmission without cable wires.
- "Backs Amateur Aid in Television Test" (June 24, 1936, page 41, column 6) discusses Farnsworth's appearance before the FCC to allow amateurs to participate in the rollout of television to the masses. Looking back on how this played out, it is clear that Farnsworth was battling big business even at this time.

There is a nice summary of Farnsworth's invention in the book *Inventing Modern America* by David E. Brown (2002, Massachusetts Institute of Technology, Cambridge, pages 58-61).

REGINALD FESSENDEN

Web Links

There are numerous sources discussing Fessenden's genius. Here are some of the longer, more in-depth stories:

"An Unsung Hero: Reginald Fessenden, the Canadian Inventor of Radio Telephony" is an excellent story that focuses on Fessenden's invention of radio. This particular story is reprinted from the *Radioscientist*, although no author or date is provided *(http://www.ewh.ieee.org/reg/7/millennium/radio/radio_unsung.html)*.

Thomas Yocum does an excellent job of discussing Fessenden's earlier work in an article titled "Reginald Fessenden: Pioneer of Wireless Radio," which can be found at *http://www.coastalguide.com/bearings/wireless01.htm*.

"Reginald Fessenden: 1866-1932" offers a nice overview of Fessenden's life and his inventions *(http://collections.ic.gc.ca/heirloom_series/volume4/42-45.htm)*.

Print Media and Additional Resources

One of the most complete and in-depth articles on Reginald Fessenden is appropriately titled "The Forgotten Father of Radio" and appears in the summer 2001 issue of *American Heritage of Invention and Technology* (volume 17, number 1, pages 40-47).

William S. Zuill has done an excellent job in pulling the story together and includes numerous photographs.

*The Cosmic Inventor: Reginald Aubrey Fessenden* by Frederick Seitz is an excellent monograph on the life of Fessenden (1999, Transactions of the American Philosophy Society, volume 89, part 6, 77 pages).

"Right Against the Wind: Fessenden and the Birth of Radio" by J. F. McEvoy is an excellent story that appears in the June/July issue of *Beaver* (volume 70, issue 3, page 43).

There are many articles on Fessenden in the *New York Times*. These are the most useful:

- "New Wireless Telephone: R. H. Fessenden Said to Have Perfected a Non-Interference Device" (April 5, 1909, page 7, column 6)
- "Fessenden Wireless 'Phone': Inventor's Backer Says He's Perfected Instrument for Talking 200 Miles" (December 23, 1909, page 10, column 2)
- "Fessenden Claims First Aerial Phone: Inventor Says Speech Was First Transmitted in 1900, and Carried Twenty-five Miles in 1905" (October 7, 1915, page 7, column 4)
- "Prof. Fessenden Buried in Bermuda: Bay State Inventor and Leader in Wireless Filed Honored at Funeral Service" (July 24, 1932, page 22, column 1)
- "Radio Loses a Pioneer" (July 31, 1932, section IX, page 7, column 1)

## PHOTOGRAPHIC FILM
### Web Links
The Internet is not a good place to do further research on this topic. The information is incomplete and very brief.

A four-paragraph summary can be found in "A History of Photography" by Robert Leggat at *http://www.rleggat.com/photo-history/history/goodwin.htm*.

### Print Media and Additional Resources
The best source on this subject is the book *Images and*

*Enterprise: Technology and the American Photographic Industry, 1839 to 1925* by Reese V. Jenkins (1975, The Johns Hopkins University Press, Baltimore). The story is scattered throughout the book, but check out pages 122–134, 248–257, and 330–337. This book is very well researched and offers excellent detail on the Goodwin patent infringement.

The fall 2001 issue of *American Heritage of Invention and Technology* (volume 17, number 2, pages 44–51) features the excellent article "The Preacher Who Beat Eastman Kodak" by Barbara Moran.

One of my favorite books of all time is *Plastic: The Making of a Synthetic Century* by Stephen Fenichell (1996, HarperCollins, New York). The first few chapters discuss the development of collodion, Parkesine and celluloid, and the ultimate invention of film. Chapter 3, "Celluloid Heroes," takes an in-depth look at the development of film, including the Goodwin patent-infringement case.

*The Story of Kodak* by Douglas Collins (1990, Harry N. Abrams, New York, pages 66–67) has a few pages of discussion on the development of flexible film within Eastman Kodak and Goodwin's invention.

The *New York Times* offers the following related stories:

- "Suit over Goodwin Kodak Film Profits" (August 10, 1914, page 5, column 7) discusses the lawsuit against Ansco by stockholders.
- "Claims Kodak Film Money" (November 26, 1914, page 18, column 1) and "Sues Inventor's Heirs" discuss the lawsuit by the family of Hugh Stevens against the Goodwin estate.
- "Film Concern in Infringement Suit" (May 21, 1915, page 19, column 1) discusses a lawsuit by Goodwin Film against Universal Film Manufacturing. In addition to the substantial Eastman Kodak settlement, this is an example of other smaller companies that also had to pay Goodwin's estate for patent infringement.

## THE PHOTOCOPIER
**Web Links**

"Chester F. Carlson" at *http://www.invent.org/hall_of_fame/27.html* provides a brief summary of Carlson's work with additional links.

"Chester F. Carlson" at *http://web.mit.edu/invent/www/inventorsA-H/carlson.html* provides brief biographical information.

**Print Media and Additional Resources**

There is no shortage of information out there on Carlson's invention.

An excellent article titled "Struggling to Become an Inventor" by Dean J. Golembeski appears on pages 40–48 of the 1997 publication *Great Inventions That Changed the World*. (This was a supplement to *American Heritage of Invention and Technology* magazine.)

Another excellent source is the book *They All Laughed* by Ira Flatow (1992, HarperCollins Publishers, New York, pages 111–118). Chapter 11 is titled "Xerox: The Machine No One Wanted."

The November 1, 1948, issue of *Time* magazine (volume 52, pages 82–83) has an article titled "Publishing: Revolution Ahead?" that describes the initial demonstration by Haloid of their new process at Manhattan's Waldorf-Astoria.

If you are curious as to how electrophotography works, the great article "Printing with Powders" appears in the June 1949 issue of *Fortune* (volume 39, pages 113–122). The basics of the process remain the same today.

Another article that appears in *Fortune* (volume 66, July 1962, pages 151–155) is titled "There Isn't Any Profit Squeeze at Xerox" and describes Xerox's meteoric rise in the early 1960s. One page is devoted to Carlson and his invention.

The following articles all appeared in the *New York Times:*

- "Electrical Photos Speed Development" (November 22, 1940, page 25, column 3) details Carlson's patent just after it was issued.
- "Inkless Process in Printing Hailed" (October 23, 1948, page 17, column 8) describes the initial demonstration by Battelle and Haloid in New York City.

- This was followed up by a second story, "Xerography Process" (October 24, 1948, Section II, page 19, column 2), the next day, describing the process and its significance.
- "Xerography Inventor Is Honored" (May 8, 1965, page 35, column 2) describes how Carlson invented the xerography process. As a result, Carlson was honored as inventor of the year by the Patent, Trademark, and Copyright Research Institute of Washington University.
- A small portion of the article "Invention, the First Step, Is Often Most Difficult" (January 8, 1968, page 138, column 1) is devoted to Carlson's work.
- An obituary titled "Chester F. Carlson Dead at Sixty-two; Invented Xerography Process" (September 20, 1968, page 47, column 1) details Carlson's life, his struggles, and his many achievements.

# Part 3: Hard to Believe

NEIL ARMSTRONG
**Web Links**
The entire text of "The Great Moon Hoax" serial can be found reprinted on The Museum of Hoaxes Web site at *http://www.muse-umofhoaxes.com/moonhoax.html*.

The Hampton Roads Central Library Web site contains the sixty-six-page story "Moon Walk 1835: Was Neil Armstrong Really the First Man on the Moon?" This story includes the text from Locke's hoax *(http://users.visi.net/~cwt/moonwalk.html)*.

I first came across this story when reading "The Great Moon Hoax of 1835" by R. J. Brown at *http://www.historybuff.com/library/refmoon.html*. This story is reprinted in other locations on the Internet.
**Print Media and Additional Resources**
It is clear that the *Daily Albany Argus* did not want to get into any hot water with its readers. When they ran the story "News from

the Moon" (September 1, 1835, page 1, column 2), they included the subheading "A Consummate Hoax" and a long paragraph discrediting the *Sun*'s publishing of it. Yet, they reprinted the entire story.

An examination of the moon hoax, along with a reprint of the serial, can be found in *The Celebrated Moon Story, Its Origin and Incidents* by William N. Griggs (Bunnell and Price, New York). Written in 1852, it is the best accounting of what happened when the story was originally published.

## ASTRONOTS
### Web Links
The Web site Bad Astronomy does an excellent job of refuting the claims made on the FOX television program. Titled "Fox TV and the Apollo Moon Hoax," this February 13, 2001, article does an excellent job of arguing against the program's logic *(http:// www.badastronomy.com/bad/tv/foxapollo.html)*.

NASA didn't keep its mouth zippered when FOX broadcast this show. Check out "The Great Moon Hoax" at *http://science.nasa.gov/ headlines/y2001/ast23feb%5F2.htm* and "Apollo Hoax Frequently Asked Questions" at *http://www.apolloarchive.com/apollo/moon_ hoax_FAQ.html.*

For a quick summary, "Proof Positive: Five Reasons to Believe We've Been to the Moon" is a great place to start *(http://www. thursdaysclassroom.com/15mar01/proofpositive.html)*.

### Print Media and Additional Resources
The May 2001 issue of the *Science Teacher* (pages 22–25) contains Paul D. Lowman Jr.'s excellent article "Evidence from Apollo: How Science Teachers Can Show Students That Humans Have Landed on the Moon."

"Faking a Hoax" by Michael Medved (*USA Today,* April 9, 2001, page A13) takes on the claims of the FOX television show that aired.

The May/June 2001 issue of the *Skeptical Inquirer* (volume 25, number 3) contains the story "Fox Special Questions Moon Landing but Not Its Own Credulities." Written by James V. Scotti, this article can be found on pages 9–12.

MAYDAY AT 41,000 FEET

**Web Links**

There is no shortage of information on this topic on the Web. Here are some of the better summaries:

"The Gimli Glider," written by Wade H. Nelson in 1997, is an excellent place to start your research. This story can be found at *http://www.frontier.net/~wadenelson/successstories/gimli.html*. If this link is inactive, the story has been reproduced by many others at various locations on the Web.

Another excellent source is "The Crash of Flight 143" by Peter Banks on the chemistry.org Web site (*http://www.acs.org*—enter *Gimli* as a search term). Included is a detailed summary of the error made in the conversion of units, which will certainly be of help to any math or science teacher looking to incorporate this into the classroom.

Be sure to check out the "Video Vault" at CBC Manitoba. At *http://www.winnipeg.cbc.ca/videovault/gimglider.html* you will find two television news reports of the incident that have been spliced together.

A very interesting Web site is AirDisaster.com *(http://www.airdisaster.com)*, which allows the reader to look up the number of crashes and corresponding survival rates of airplanes. You can search by type of airplane, manufacturer, and airline. While there is no detailed explanation of the Gimli disaster here, it does offer excellent statistics and two images of the Gimli Glider itself.

**Print Media and Additional Resources**

The most complete work on this topic is *Freefall: A True Story* by William and Marilyn Mona Hoffer (1989, St. Martin's Press, New York). This book is very well researched but contains a lot of filler. It was clearly written with the intention of being made into a movie (which it was). If you stick strictly to the chapters on the cockpit and control tower, you will be able to bypass all of the filler and still get the complete story.

## SIR ALFRED
**Web Links**

The July 14, 1999, Associated Press story by Susannah Patton titled "It's Time to Fly for Paris Airport's Longtime Refugee" discusses Nasseri's situation at the time. It also has a brief overview of how he got into this predicament *(http://archives.seattletimes.nwsource.com/cgi-bin/texis.cgi/web/vortex/display?slug=airp&date=19990923).*

The story is examined in detail on the Urban Legends Reference Pages at *http://www.snopes.com/travel/airline/airport.htm.*

*The Straight Dope* author Cecil Adams examines Nasseri's problems in his August 20, 1999, story "Has a Guy Been Stuck in the Paris Airport Since 1988 for Lack of the Right Papers?" *(http://www.straightdope.com/classics/a990820.html).*

**Print Media and Additional Resources**

One of the earliest stories on Nasseri's dilemma can be found in the *Wall Street Journal* article "The Man Without a Country Resides at Charles de Gaulle." Written by Judith Valente, this story can be found on page A1 of the October 7, 1994, issue (volume 224, number 69).

Elizabeth Neuffer has written a very detailed story on the subject. Titled "A Man Without a Country," the article can be found in the December 25, 1997, issue of the *Boston Globe* (page A1).

## THE U.S. CAMEL CORPS
**Web Links**

Ellen Jacobs has done a nice job in the preparation of "The U.S. Camel Corps" at *http://www.drumbarracks.org/Camel%20Corps.html.* This site is a great place to start your research into the topic.

"U.S. Camel Corps Remembered in Quartzsite, Arizona" by Chuck Woodbury provides a good overview of the use of camels in the U.S. military *(http://www.outwestnewspaper.com/camels.html).*

**Print Media and Additional Resources**

I originally found this story in my collection of old hardbound *American Heritage* magazines. "The Red Ghost" by Robert Froman appears in the April 1961 issue, beginning on page 35.

*Uncle Sam's Camels* (edited by Lewis Burt Lesley, 1929, Harvard University Press, Cambridge) contains the journal of May Humphrey Stacey, who participated in the experimental camel program. The book is also supplemented by Beale's camel report to the government.

## THE MIRACLE MAN
### Web Links
"White Caps and Bull Doozers, or Will Purvis" by Pamela J. Gibbs is an excellent retelling of the Will Purvis story. This excellent story can be found on the Mississippi Local History Network at *http://www.usgennet.org/usa/ms/state/outlaws/* (2000).

### Print Media and Additional Resources
The best source on this subject is the *True Life Story of Will Purvis* by Frances Williams Griffith (1935, Booster Publishing Company, Purvis, Miss.). Although poorly edited and brief in length, this fifty-eight-page book is basically Will Purvis telling the story in his own words.

An additional well-researched story is the chapter "Will Purvis: Mississippi" from the book *Convicting the Innocent: Errors in Criminal Justice* by Edwin M. Borchard (1970, Da Capo Press, New York, pages 210–217). This is a reprint of the first edition of the book, originally published in 1932.

Another good source is *When Men Play God: The Fallacy of Capital Punishment* by Eugene B. Block (1983, Cragmont Publications, San Francisco). The Will Purvis story is part of the chapter titled "Are Innocents Executed?" on pages 55–61.

A six-paragraph summary can be found in the book *Mysteries of the Unexplained,* which has been compiled by *Reader's Digest* (1982, The Reader' Digest Association, Inc., pages 270–271). The story "The Unknotted Noose" features images of both Purvis and the check that the state of Mississippi cut him.

The Friday, February 9, 1894, issue of the *New York Times* contains the article "Had to Postpone the Hanging: Convicted Murderer Fell to the Ground from a Broken Noose" (page 12, column 1). This short article has many of the facts in the case misstated but does confirm the actual date of the botched hanging.

THE 1904 OLYMPICS

Print Media and Additional Resources

The excellent book *Oops!* by Paul Kirchner (1996, Rhino Records, Los Angeles, pages 106–107) offers a fairly detailed summary of the St. Louis Marathon.

Two articles from the *New York Times* were valuable in the preparation of this story: The first, titled "Olympic Games of 1904," appears in the Wednesday, July 20, 1904, issue and summarizes the preparations made for the Olympic Games. Since readers probably were not familiar with the Olympics at the time, the article details a history of the games. The second article, titled "American Runner Wins," was featured in the August 31, 1904, issue on page 5. This story details the marathon and Lorz's eventual disqualification.

The May 15, 1996, issue of *Newsday* features an article titled "Olympics in the Political Arena: Clinton to Be No Stranger to Atlanta," which profiles the role that United States presidents have played in the Olympic Games. A brief summary of the 1904 games is given.

If you are looking for details, details, and even more details on all of the Olympics, be sure to check out *The Complete Book of the Olympics* by David Wallechinsky. There are many updated editions of this book, which is published by Penguin Books.

An excellent chapter on the 1904 Olympics can be found in the book *An Approved History of the Olympic Games* by Bill Henry (1976, G. P. Putnam's Sons, New York, pages 50–57).

Another excellent book is *All That Glitters Is Not Gold: An Irreverent Look at the Olympic Games* by William O. Johnson Jr. (1972, G. P. Putnam's Son's, New York, pages 120–127).

And yet another is *The Story of the Olympic Games* by John Kieran, Arthur Daley, and Pat Jordan (1977, J. B. Lippincott Company, Philadelphia, pages 39–49).

Finally, if you are in the market for a big, colorful book filled with pictures, check out *Chronicles of the Olympics, 1896–1996*, published by DK Publishing, Inc. (1996, Boston, pages 24–27).

# Part 4: It All Comes with Being Human

## THE BATH SCHOOL DISASTER
**Web Links**

Thanks to the hard work of a few people, this story is very well documented on the Internet and a trip to the library is hardly necessary. Any research into this topic should start with a visit to *http://freepages.history.rootsweb.com/~bauerle/disaster.htm*. Here you will find links to a great collection of images and newspaper and magazine articles, and to additional Web sites. Excellent site!

Mark Gado has written the e-text "Hell Comes to Bath: America's Worst School Violence Ever." The story can be found on The Crime Library Web site at *http://www.crimelibrary.com/serial7/bath/*.

## OTA BENGA
**Web Links**

"Ota Benga: The Man Who Was Put on Display in the Zoo!" by Jerry Bergman, Ph.D., is an excellent summary on-line of this poor man's life *(http://www.onehumanrace.com/docs/ota_benga.asp)*.

**Print Media and Additional Resources**

If you would like to do further research on this topic, get your hands on a copy of the book *Ota Benga: The Pygmy in the Zoo* by Phillips Verner Bradford and Harvey Blume (1992, St. Martin's Press, New York). Bradford and Blume's telling of the story seems to go a bit beyond what the actual evidence shows, but the back of this book is filled with a large number of press clippings from the *New York Times* and other sources.

One of the first stories that I ever read on Ota Benga was "The Man in the Zoo" by Geoffrey C. Ward, which appears in the October 1992 issue of *American Heritage* (volume 43, number 6, pages 12–14).

## MURDEROUS MARY

**Web Links**

Joan Vannorsdall Schroeder has written the excellent article "There's a Skeleton in a Train Yard in East Tennessee," which appears on the Blue Ridge Country Online Web site *(http://www. blueridgecountry.com/elephant/elephant.html)*.

The August 2000 *Internet Web Guide Magazine* contains the story "Big Mary, Hanged for Murder or Vigilantism Against Pachyderms in East Tennessee?" and includes the famous photograph of Mary's hanging *(http://www.internetwebguide.com/mag2000/aug/mary.asp)*.

While this story is factual, there is a nice summary of it found on the SciFi Network's Web site. Scoot over to *http://www. scifi.com/scifi.con/word/gothic/elephant.html* to read "Welcome to Weirdsville: Never Forget" by M. Christian.

**Print Media and Additional Resources**

The hard-to-find book *The Day They Hung the Elephant* by Charles Edwin Price (1992, The Overmountain Press, Johnson City, Tenn.) is the best place to start when researching this story further. Copies can be purchased through your local bookseller or through interlibrary loan at your local library. At forty-four pages, this is light reading, but it is the most complete work on the hanging of Mary.

## CHARLES PONZI

**Web Links**

There is certainly no shortage of information on Ponzi's scheme out there on the Internet. Just use your favorite search engine to discover a wealth of information.

Be sure to check out the "Charles K. Ponzi Website." Mark C. Knutson has done some excellent research on Ponzi and has included the text of several federal documents, including Ponzi's telegram to President Coolidge *(http://www.mark-knutson.com/)*.

**Print Media and Additional Resources**

The newspapers from the 1920s are, without a doubt, the best sources available. Be prepared, however. This was quite the sensational story in its day and the scandal was followed by the press for years. Nearly 150 articles were printed in the *New York Times* between 1920 and 1930 alone. The Boston papers are certainly excellent sources, although they are not typically found in as many libraries as the *New York Times*.

One of the best-detailed summaries on the Ponzi scheme can be found in the article "Bubble, Bubble—No Toil, No Trouble" by Francis Russell. The story can be found in the February 1973 issue of *American Heritage* magazine (volume 24, number 2, pages 74–80). The author has done an excellent job of sorting through the mounds of stories and putting them together into one cohesive story.

## THE NEW ENGLISH

### Web Links

Craig Ganzer has transcribed many excerpts of the book and has posted them on his Web site Ganz's World! Links are provided to the various categories of common words, phrases, and dialogues. He has done a nice job here and, while not complete, it will save you the effort of trying to track down a copy of the book *(http://www.fragment.com/~ganz/spoke.html)*.

If you wish to purchase a reprint of this book, it has been published by McSweeney's and can be ordered through their on-line store at *http://www.mcsweeneys.net/2002/04/01collins.html*.

There are a number of short discussions on this unusual book on the Internet. A quick search should find numerous matches.

### Print Media and Additional Resources

I was able to locate an 1883 copy of *The New Guide of the Conversation in Portuguese and English* (J. R. Osgood and Company, Boston) at the New York State Library, but reprints are more easily found. The most popular reprint is the Dover Publications version (1969, New York), which is available through many libraries across the United States. Libraries may have the author listed as either Pedro Carolino, José de Fonseca, or Mark Twain, so an initial computer search may not produce results.

# Part 5: Hmmm...

<u>MURPHY'S LAW</u>
**Web Links**

One thousand and five schoolchildren in the United Kingdom participated in a study to see if toast really does land buttered side down. After almost 10,000 tries, they answered this question conclusively. It lands buttered side down 62 percent of the time. You can read background on the study, the experimental design, the data, and conclusions in the *Sum Newspaper* at *http://www.mathsyear2000.org/thesum/issue8/*.

"Murphy's Law" *(http://bordeaux.uwaterloo.ca/biology447/modules/intro/MurphysScience.html)* offers a brief overview of Robert Matthews's ideas, along with simplified diagrams. Very basic but excellent to help kids understand.

The Australian Broadcasting Corporation offers "Great Moments in Science" by Karl S. Kruszelnicki. Here you will find another story aptly tilted "Murphy's Law," which offers a nice discussion of who Murphy was and how his law came to be. Use your Real Audio player to listen to the radio version *(http://www.abc.net.au/science/k2/moments/gmis9906.htm)*.

As you probably already know, Murphy's Law is not the only law out there. Just point your browser to Roman Koch's Murphy's Law page *(http://www.romankoch.ch/capslock/murphy.htm*, 1999) for over 100 of them, ranging from the airplane law to Zymurgy's first law of systems dynamics. My personal favorite is Weber's Definition, which I will leave for you to check out. . . .

**Print Media and Additional Resources**

The best place to start your research would be with the April 1997 *Scientific American* article "The Science of Murphy's Law" by Robert A. J. Matthews (pages 88–91). Definitely well worth reading.

Matthews also published "Tumbling Toast, Murphy's Law and the Fundamental Constants," which can be found in the *European Journal of Physics* (June 1995, volume 15, pages 172–176). Warning:

This paper is not written for the layman. It includes a small amount of calculus and statistics but can still provide good information.

Matthews has also posted some of his journal articles on-line for reference. You can either go to the library and hunt these articles down, or point your browser to the following addresses: "Murphy's Law of Maps" (*Teaching Statistics*, 1997, volume 19, pages 34–35) located at *http://ourworld.compuserve.com/homepages/rajm/mapfull.htm* and "Knotted Rope: A Topological Example of Murphy's Law" (*Mathematics Today*, 1997, volume 33, pages 82–84, 85) located at *http://ourworld.compuserve.com/homepages/rajm/knotfull.htm.*

## ARBOR DAY
**Web Links**

The Web is loaded with excellent information on Arbor Day. Yet, almost everything that you would need to know can be found at the National Arbor Day Foundation *(http://www.arborday.org/).* This site has a wealth of information and can help anybody that is interested in planting a tree for Arbor Day.

**Print Media and Additional Resources**

Much of the information presented in this story comes from Chatham Central School's application for the oldest Arbor Day tree in New York State. This contest was held in 1988 to commemorate the 100th anniversary of the celebration in the state. This material is on file at the school's district office. A special thanks to Ann Flanagan for help in finding this material.

## THE ELECTRIC PICKLE
**Web Links**

One of the best sites on the topic is Lori's Chemistry Page at *http://www.geocities.com/CapeCanaveral/Launchpad/6603/glowing.html*, which features great photographs of the experiment plus setup instructions. Should you choose to do this experiment, please read the directions carefully!

D. Brouse, D. Brouse, T. Brouse, and S. Mukherjee have produced the scientific article "The Pickle as Will and Idea," which is located at *http://ygraine.membrane.com/hubris/notes/electric_pickle.html*. Don't worry about the science on this site: This page has actual videos of the experiments. (The only thing that they couldn't capture was the horrific smell.)

One of the best references on the subject is the Digital Western Research Laboratory paper titled "Characterization of Organic Illumination Systems." It is available on-line at the Compaq Web site *(http://www.research.compaq.com/wrl/techreports/abstracts/ TN-13.html)*. With an April 1, 1989, publication date, keep in mind that this was really written as an April Fool's joke, but for such a ludicrous topic, the science is very well done.

**Print Media and Additional Resources**

Be sure to check out the March 1993 issue of the *Journal of Chemical Education* for the article "Tested Demonstrations: Sodium D Line Emission from Pickles" by George L. Gilbert (volume 70, number 3, pages 250–251).

Writer David George Gordon has written an interesting article titled "Mad or Rad: Electric Pickles." This story was part of the ABC News Web site but is no longer available.

HIROO ONODA

**Web Links**

The Web site No Surrender: Japanese Holdouts details Onoda and other soldiers that did not know that the war was over. It also features a links page, which is a great starting point for exploring the Web *(http://www.wanpela.com/holdouts/)*.

Be sure to check out the *Giant Robot* magazine article titled "Hide and Seek." One section is devoted to "Rambo Onoda" *(http://www.giantrobot.com/issues/issue07/hs/hsmain.html)*.

**Print Media and Additional Resources**

The best source available on this subject is Hiroo Onoda's autobiography *No Surrender: My Thirty-Year War*. This book was originally published in 1974 but has since been reissued and is available at many bookstores.

The *New York Times* offers these articles:

- "Two Japanese Holdouts Shot in the Philippines" (October 21, 1972, page 41, column 2)
- "Japanese Official Found in Philippines After Twenty-nine Years" (March 11, 1974, page 3, column 1)
- "Marcos Extols Japanese Straggler, Returns Sword" (March 12, 1974, page 3, column 5)
- "Soldier's Return from Thirty Years in Jungle Stirs Japanese Deeply" (March 13, 1974, page 1, column 1)
- "Japanese, Long in Jungle, in Fine Health" (April 24, 1974, page 1, column 6)
- "Thirty Years of Hiding in Jungle Were Foolish, Japanese Say" (June 19, 1974, page 1, column 7)
- "Notes on People" (October 24, 1974, page 50, column 1)
- "Ex-Japanese Soldier Unhappy After Years in Philippine Jungle" (November 29, 1974, page 46, column 1)

## RUBBER DUCKIES
Web Links

The Web is filled with information related to this story, particularly in reference to the rubber duckies and Nike sneakers that were floating around.

Dr. Ebbesmeyer maintains the Beachcombers' Alert Web site, which is a great place to learn about things afloat in our oceans. The site does not appear to be updated frequently but contains a wealth of useful information *(http://beachcombers.org/)*.

Print Media and Additional Resources

"Treasures of the Tide" by Michael McRae appears in the fall 1997 issue of *Forbes*. This one-page article starts on page 9 and discusses the life of Steve McLeod, a beachcomber that rises each day to collect whatever may have washed up on the Oregon shoreline. The story goes on to discuss the research of Ebbesmeyer.

The following articles on the stuff washing up on our shores are just a brief sampling of the many available on the topic:

"Lots of Legos May Turn Up on Your Beach" by Charles W. Petit appears in the April 20, 1998, issue of *U.S. News and World Report* (volume 124, issue 15, page 59).

"Tracking the Treasures, Toys and Trash that Wash Up on the Nation's Shores" by Karen Westerberg Reves appears in the June/July issue of *National Wildlife* (volume 37, issue 4, page 74).

"King of Currents Tracks Ocean Flotsam" by David George Gordon appears in the February 12, 1999, issue of *Current Science* (volume 84, issue 11, page 6).

Charlene P. Nelson has written "Shoes Overboard!" which can be found in the March 1995 issue of *Highlights for Children* (volume 50, issue 3, page 16).